THE ART OF INQUIRY

THE ART OF INQUIRY

A DEPTH PSYCHOLOGICAL PERSPECTIVE

SECOND, REVISED EDITION

JOSEPH COPPIN
ELIZABETH NELSON

SPRING PUBLICATIONS, INC.
PUTNAM, CONNECTICUT

Published by Spring Publications, Inc.
www.springpublications.com

Second, revised edition 2005
Second Printing 2007

Inquiries should be addressed to:
Spring Publications, Inc.
P.O. Box 230212
New York, N.Y. 10023

Designed by white.room productions, New York

Printed in Canada

Library of Congress Cataloging-in-Publication Data

Coppin, Joseph.
  The art of inquiry : a depth psychological perspective / Joseph Coppin,
  Elizabeth Nelson.— 2nd rev. ed.
      p. cm.
  Includes bibliographical references and index.
  ISBN-13: 978-0-88214-559-4 (pbk. : alk. paper)
  ISBN-10: 0-88214-559-2 (pbk. : alk. paper)
  1. Psychology—Research—Methodology. I. Nelson, Elizabeth. II. Title.
  BF76.5.C666 2005
  150'.72—dc22

                          2005004417

  ∞ The paper used in this publication meets the minimum requirements of the
American National Standard for Information Sciences — Permanence of Paper
for Printed Library Materials, ANSI Z39.48-1992.

CONTENTS

PREFACE

The original idea for this book arose from our experience in the class-room, teaching research to students in depth psychology. A persis-tent question presented itself: How does a researcher discover, explore, and write about a topic of interest in a way that is true to the psyche? Another related question was how does the psyche shape and guide the research process? In attempting an answer, we realized our own research in depth psychology had been passionate, creative, and meaningful — quite unlike the stories we heard from other researchers, even from other psychologists. What is it that accounts for the exceptional experience of depth psychological inquiry at its best? Is it possible to articulate what the research experience is like when it is centered on and guided by the psyche? If so, can we express our findings in a manner that is both philo-sophically provocative and practically useful to anyone writing a book, a thesis, a dissertation, or an essay? The answer at the time was a resound-ing "yes." Beginnings are often bold; and so were we.

Because we write in service to the psyche it is good to begin with some common understanding of what we mean by the word, *psyche*. This is a large enough task to warrant its own chapter, which is the substance of Chapter 3, *Philosophical Commitments of Depth Psychology*. Let us say here that the psyche is the great repository of ideas, images, emotions, urges, and desires that appear in the world, whether its source is personal or collective, conscious or unconscious. This is a depth view of the psyche. It is unlike more limited definitions that often equate the psyche with the personal mind.

A great deal of inquiry into the human situation is conducted using approaches and methods that do not account for this larger view of the psyche. Such inquiry may provide valuable information, but it is inherently unpsychological. This is a matter of obvious concern for students of psychology. It also is increasingly important to anyone whose work touches on the human situation. It has become painfully clear to many people that our understanding of each other and ourselves is psychologically naive. In light of globalization, which attempts to disguise yet paradoxically intensifies humanity's cultural, social, political, religious, and geographical differences, such naivety is not helpful in addressing critical problems. A more complex understanding of humanity and the world, and ways to gain that understanding, are essential. A depth psychological perspective fosters meaningful work that is deep, complex, and worldly.

In calling our book *The Art of Inquiry* we are also inviting a departure from the modern tendency to split science from art and knowledge from aesthetics. Art is a realm that has never needed to neutralize the character of the artist in the way that natural science has for so long sought to neutralize the character of the scientist. In art there is a continual flow of being into doing and doing into being that affirms the idea that works of art are essentially human. Works of art also are intentionally particular; their value lies in their "eachness." Our book applies the artistic sensibility to the work of inquiry. Though *The Art of Inquiry* departs from conventional thinking, it is not as revolutionary as it might have been 50 years ago. Post-modern thought, in its ongoing critique of positivism, has challenged individuals to reflect upon what they know and how they know it. Many people are more willing to recognize that facts have never been enough, nor have they been all that powerful in guiding thought and action. The devotion to reason has, in modern times, favored facts over aesthetic approaches to knowing. This is changing. Thoughtful individuals are willing to acknowledge that one's world view and the actions that proceed from it are best when informed by art in the broadest sense. We appreciate that change and have experienced a growing desire to address it systematically by offering a text that gives inquiring minds an alternative to the typical approach to research methodology.

What are these differences? To begin with, this is not a book on method. We discuss method and its role in creative work, but we take the position that method always has a reductive tendency. It reduces the phenomena of the world in order to describe them more clearly. Reduction is consistently harsh on psychological phenomena which, by their nature, are fluid, multiple, and complex. Artists whose work is faithful to this complexity tend to be better at representing psychological phenomena than psychologists are. So we take on this challenge not by producing yet another method but by examining the relationships between art, inquiry, method, and the psyche. We look at this mixture historically and philosophically and arrive at a place where it is more important to articulate *moves* instead of methods. Whereas method can reduce, constrain, or fix psychological phenomena, moves are dynamic processes of inquiry that correspond to the fluid nature of the psyche.

Looking ahead, Chapter 1, *Inquiry and the Care of the Soul*, provides a deeper introduction to the book and establishes inquiry in a tradition centered on the soul. We argue that inquiry is a natural activity of the soul, and as such it crosses boundaries of time, culture, and space. The chapter defines psychological inquiry as a way of approaching all inquiry from a psychologically adept perspective, not merely as an approach to research in psychology.

Chapter 2, *The Historical Contexts of Psychological Inquiry*, examines psychological inquiry in the context of critical philosophy, the tradition that explores the gaps between theories of experience and the actual experiences of living. The chapter traces the historical development of qualitative research as a genealogy of ideas, a myth of origin, rather than the factual historical account of qualitative research. This approach emphasizes the psyche's own penchant for narrative and the principle that all truth, especially historical truth, is partial and contextual.

Chapter 3, *Philosophical Commitments of Depth Psychology*, is a succinct tour through eight key ideas that distinguish the discipline of depth psychology from other disciplines and other branches of psychology. Some of these commitments are obvious but need to be stated anyway, for instance, "The psyche is real." Others are less obvious yet have profound repercussions for any creative project. For instance, what might it mean to the inquiry process that the psyche is symptomatic, or complex, or more-than-personal? We explain these ideas and suggest answers to the questions in this chapter.

Chapter 4, *The Moves of Psychological Inquiry*, discusses the role of method in all knowledge claims, including how method shapes a person's vision of what is real, and makes a distinction between the methods and the moves, or processes, of inquiry. It describes some of the key moves that make any creative project more psychological, including moves of structure, content, and language. In providing an appreciative criticism of methodology, and inviting the use of specific moves that respond to the criticisms, we shift our focus from the realms of philosophy and theory into the realm of practice.

Chapter 5, *Applying the Moves of Psychological Inquiry to Scholarly Research*, sustains the pragmatic emphasis of Chapter 4 and focuses on a particular kind of inquiry: scholarly research. It outlines the phases of the scholarly research process, and describes how the moves of psychological inquiry fit within these phases. Chapter 5 helps readers move towards a completed project, using stories and examples illustrating some of the common challenges and anxieties of psychological inquiry.

Chapter 6, *Honoring the Spirit of Play*, takes the art of inquiry beyond the bounds of scholarly research to explore how inquiry can become a way of living. It is a reflection on the archetypal child who has guided this book, and who has been a central figure in the historical development of depth psychology. In musing upon the child, it becomes apparent that one important route to living a psychological life is to adopt the curious, playful, eager and daring attitude of the child who delights in discovering the world. Thus this chapter honors the spirit of play and discovery when it poses such questions as: How does inquiry lead to care of the soul? How can the individual express the commitments of depth psychology in daily life? Which shifts are necessary to fully participate in the *anima mundi*? How does inquiry affect one's daily habits, relationships, work, and the *telos* of one's life? This last chapter demonstrates the richness of the depth psychological perspective and affirms the joy of living such questions.

A NOTE ON VOICE

Throughout this text we have chosen to represent our work personally and speak as collaborators, using the pronoun *we*. It is personal in the sense that this project has been our personal focus for some time. What is said here represents that personal participation as much as it does any theoretical or historical truth. The personal voice, rather than devaluing the substance of our thoughts, steers clear of the fiction of the omniscient narrator so common in academic writing. But the pronoun *we* is also used to reflect our collaboration. This book is a true collaboration. Both of us entered into an ongoing participation with the ideas it contains, we each made our contributions, and we have been transformed by the process. Authorship is therefore deliciously ambiguous, but we accept full responsibility nonetheless.

I

INQUIRY AND THE CARE OF THE SOUL

At some point in our lives nearly all of us have been naturally inquisitive. "Why?" is a favorite question of toddlers, and in their voices one hears a genuine curiosity rarely satisfied with that staple adult answer, "Because." Depending on how much time and energy one has, a child's endless curiosity can be tedious, annoying, or a thing of wonder. This book is written on behalf of the wondrous nature of inquiry. Its guiding spirit is the archetypal child, who continues asking questions for the sheer delight of exploration and discovery.

Inquiry, as we present it in this book, is more than asking questions. It is an active, reciprocal relationship with the world that can last through the completion of a creative project but can also endure for a lifetime. This relationship is often expressed in two distinctive postures that anyone engaged in inquiry can adopt — seeking knowledge and being receptive to knowledge that seeks us. We intentionally use the word "posture" to suggest that seeking and receiving involve the mind and body equally, and therefore express the person's whole being. These two postures are the *yang* and *yin* of inquiry; each enriches and gives meaning to the other. First we'll discuss seeking.

Seeking knowledge is the *yang* of inquiry. It is an active choice to initiate the learning process. When one pursues a question or an area of interest, one moves toward it in the same way that a lover leans her whole body toward the beloved. Posture in such moments says it all: the lover is eager, curious, and interested. In pausing to reflect upon this experience, it is evident that it offers two distinct pleasures. The first pleasure is having a lover; the second pleasure is being a lover. The pleasures of love are similar to the pleasures of active, engaged inquiry. Both intensify the person's relationship to the world as it exists beyond the boundaries of the mind and flesh, so that the world, and one's connection to it, become more truly alive. A person pursuing a question thrums with the vitality of energized engagement.

Some readers may object to the comparison between a person assertively pursuing knowledge and a person in love. Aren't they qualitatively different? Aren't we being a bit over the top when we compare one experience to the other? No, not really. This analogy simply describes a fundamental characteristic of the human psyche, which is the desire to know and to be known. For tens of thousands of years, well before the advent of written history, human beings have recorded this desire in cave paintings and carved deities that hint at the awe they felt when encountering the immensity and grandeur of the cosmos. As creatures granted with the gift of reflective consciousness, human beings seek meaning in the depths of space — both inner space as well as outer space.

In comparing the inquirer to the lover we also are standing on firm philosophical footing that has endured in written history for more than 2500 years. In the dialogues of Plato, love is a quest, a uniquely human longing to see and know what is great and enduring instead of remaining satisfied with the illusory and ephemeral. Plato, speaking through his teacher and literary protagonist Socrates, named this longing *eros,* which for classical Greeks was a *theos* (god) of great power. Simply, the philosopher loves wisdom. This meaning is suggested by the etymology of the word *philosophy,* that is, lover (*philo*) of *sophia,* the Greek word for wisdom. Socrates and Plato were not the first to consider themselves lovers of wisdom. Scholars credit Pythagoras with the origin of the term philosophy and trace many of Plato's concepts, including his ideas about reality, to Pythagorean roots. Yet it was Socrates, in his defense speech before the Athenian tribunal who is best remembered for establishing just what the pursuit of wisdom really amounts to. In words that have an astonishing contemporary relevance, he admonishes the Athenians for their priorities. "Are you not ashamed that you give your attention to acquiring as much money as possible, and similarly with reputation and honor, and give no attention or thought to truth and understanding and the perfection of your soul?"[1] A short while later Socrates declares that the pursuit of goodness and self-examination is "the best sort of thing a man can do, and that life without this sort of examination is not worth living."[2] Human beings, uniquely endowed with the capacity to think for themselves and to love wisdom in this active, devoted way, are obligated to use this capacity to the utmost. Examination, or inquiry, is essential to a meaningful human life.

The dialogues of Plato make it clear that no person can be called wise, not even Socrates. In the *Phaedrus* we learn that *wise* is an "epithet proper only to a god," which is why the best human being can only be a "lover of wisdom."[3] Thus inquiry is fundamentally an expression of piety, one of the five Socratic virtues. It demonstrates reverence for what the gods alone possess and, by implication, for the sacred faculty within human beings, the soul. Philosophy is erotic longing for the other, an other who will always remain just beyond reach. There are other reverberations in this word *philosophy* worth mentioning any discussion of inquiry, eros, and wisdom. The Greek word *sophia* calls to mind the ancient feminine incarnation of Wisdom, Sophia. From an archetypal perspective, the love of wisdom is desire and longing for the goddess Wisdom in one of her many incarnations. Wisdom symbolizes "the highest quality of the soul" that can blossom into an understanding of all things and "soar . . . between the dimensions of earth and heaven."[4] Wisdom has come to include "many related ideas to which we now give separate names: truth, compassion, insight, knowledge, understanding, justice, divine law expressed in human institutions, and the whole ethical realm of human endeavor."[5] Wisdom also is an archetype of relationship and participation, exactly the sort of emphasis one would expect from someone who identifies himself as a lover of wisdom.

If seeking knowledge is the *yang* of inquiry, being receptive to knowledge is the *yin*. Like seeking, receptivity also is a distinctive posture in which qualities other than assertiveness and eagerness are paramount. These qualities include patience, openness and acceptance. One listens more than speaks and becomes a gatherer of knowledge, experience, and insight. To be receptive, it is crucial to develop peripheral awareness and learn to diffuse the attention over a broad area, like a fisherman who casts a net across the surface of the sea and watches it sink toward the depths and flow with the undulations of the current. Adopting the *yín* posture in inquiry means developing an ear for subtle nuance and an eye for what is partly obscure: underneath, within, behind, or just around the corner.

Receiving, the *yín* of inquiry, may easily be confused with doing nothing. Yet ask any zoologist with field experience, someone who has waited silently in the wilderness to study an animal, bird, or reptile, and he will confess how much effort this posture requires. Patient, attentive observation can be very difficult. The zoologist practices stillness so the shy creature he is observing will emerge from hiding and occupy its habitat without alarm or wariness. Likewise, the person engaged in inquiry adopts a similar stillness, allowing knowledge, insight or wisdom to come forth of its own accord. In such situations, the active achieving tendency of the ego must take a backseat and learn quiescence. One surrenders the need to seek or pursue, to put one's self forward, or to champion one's own ideas. Instead, researchers make room for another, trusting that the silence immediately following the stillness of their own voice is full rather than empty. Those who track the images of a dream through the wilderness of the unconscious know this well. For the purpose and meaning of the dream to appear, dreamers and dream analysts must practice an alert, active receptivity in which patience is paramount. It is only then that they can discover who is visiting and what wants attention.

The receptive *yín* posture often provokes fear or anxiety. It can seem unproductive especially in a culture that values achievement. It can seem counterproductive to someone who has undertaken a creative task and expects to see a steady accumulation of visible accomplishments. Writers and artists who have more experience with lengthy projects know that surrender and patience are essential to creativity. The poet Rainer Maria Rilke uses the metaphor of childbirth to describe this posture:

> Everything is gestation and then birthing. To let each impression and each embryo of a feeling come to completion, entirely in itself, in the dark, in the unsayable, the unconscious, beyond the reach of one's own understanding, and with deep humility and patience to wait for the hour when a new clarity is born: this alone is what it means to live as an artist: in understanding as in creating.[6]

A receptive, patient *yin* posture so useful in inquiry is as natural as the active *yang* posture of seeking knowledge. The need for both styles arises organically out of the nature of the psyche and its two poles of awareness: unconsciousness and consciousness. The two poles dramatize the dialectical nature of the psyche, where shadow is the counterpart to light, forgetting is the counterpart to remembering, confusion is the counterpart to clarity, and diffuse awareness is the counterpart to focused intention. In the art of inquiry, the *yin* of receiving information, knowledge, or insight is the counterpart to *yang* of seeking. Awareness of such oppositions augments knowledge by challenging people to be more whole-minded in their approach to knowing and more humble in the face of all that can be known. To quote Heraclitus, "it is the opposite which is good for us."

INQUIRY AS AN ART

It should be evident by now that inquiry as we are defining it is not simply a set of procedures to follow to get from point A, "the question," to point B, "the answer." Though we will go on to explain the process of inquiry and offer procedural guidelines, even these guidelines speak as much about attitude as they do about processes. Furthermore, no two people can follow these procedures and expect identical results. The person cannot be extracted from the work, nor would we want this to happen. Inquiry is a relational art in which researchers and the object of their interest influence one another.

In fact, inquiry is more art than science for many reasons. Perhaps the best explanation is found in the following passage from Freud's lectures on psychoanalysis wherein he staunchly defends its scientific basis or world view (*Weltanschauung*). Psychoanalysis, he says,

> Is quite unfit to construct a *Weltanschauung* of its own: it must accept the scientific one . . . It asserts that there are no sources of knowledge of the universe other than the intellectual working-over of carefully scrutinized observations — in other words, what we call research — and alongside of it no knowledge derived from revelation, intuition or divination. [7]

We refer to Freud the scientist to take issue with him. The art of inquiry presumes and even insists on a wider array of knowledge sources than those which science, at least in Freud's definition, is willing to credit. Certainly observation is a valuable source of information and we wouldn't want to dispense with it, even if that were possible. But observation is only one source of information and careful scrutiny is only one style of working with observable phenomena. Contrary to what Freud says, great insight and wisdom can come through revelation, intuition, and divination. Moreover, the *art* of inquiry lies in developing and integrating each of these information sources and allowing their fusion to enrich the quest for knowledge.

In Freud's defense, it was justified to portray psychoanalysis as a science, especially in the early part of the century. His overarching concern was to establish psychoanalysis as a legitimate and separate discipline offering clear, substantive theories and a systematic praxis. Freud wanted other medical and scientific experts to take psychoanalysis seriously and to take up and expand upon his provisional conclusions, revising them on the basis of further experience. In Freud's view, the methodology of empirical science was the best way to accomplish this. Yet as a science, Freud's fledgling discipline immediately encountered an insurmountable problem. The psyche is fathomless, as Heraclitus said. Though it is commonplace to compare the unconscious to the ocean — a symbol that suggests its vastness, fluidity, and mystery — even this metaphor ultimately is inadequate. Explorers can and have charted the ocean floor, but no explorer of the psyche will ever reach the psyche's limit, regardless of how systematic or thorough the method. One simply cannot serve up the psyche to the scrutiny of consciousness. Thankfully it will always remain virgin territory, a wilderness that cannot be tamed. The psyche is fundamentally immeasurable and therefore impossible to quantify or fully define, despite Freud's assurances to the contrary: "Where id was, there ego shall be. It is a work of culture — not unlike the draining of the Zuider Zee."[8] Though the psyche, particularly its unconscious dimension, does not lend itself to the exactness sought by science, it can be studied systematically and empirically, which is what Freud set out to do, and did.

Even if psychoanalysis fails as an exact science, its great value is un-
diminished. Furthermore, Freud's campaign to make psychology a legitimate discipline succeeded beyond his wildest dreams. Freud reminded
humanity that symptoms and dreams have meaning — they are ways the
unconscious beckons people to be curious and inquisitive — and what the
person doesn't know and cannot see has enormous influence. Since his
death in 1939, psychology has become a popular field of scholarly study
and psychological thinking has embedded itself in culture becoming, in
the words of W. H. Auden's poetic tribute to Freud, "a whole climate of
opinion."[9] Over time, Freud's theories and methods have been critiqued,
modified and transformed into a rich array of therapeutic practices. Each
of these practices is distinctive. All of them demonstrate a fundamental
commitment to the value of inquiry. It is for this reason that we occasionally will use clinical examples to illustrate a point. We invite the reader to
consider the therapeutic setting as metaphor for the way individuals can
engage the world, with patient listening and active questing alternating
with one another in the search for depth, substance, and meaning.

DEPTH PSYCHOLOGY AS A PERSPECTIVE

At this point it is perhaps appropriate to answer another question that is
clamoring for attention: Why a depth psychological perspective? What
unique insights does depth psychology as a discipline have to offer to
someone engaged in inquiry? There are many answers to this question,
which will become evident in Chapter 3, *Philosophical Commitments of Depth
Psychology*. A brief introduction to some key ideas here will suffice.

Depth psychology is a formal discipline of inquiry. In the last century
it has taken up the gauntlet that Socrates laid down 2,500 years ago. Classical Athens bears some remarkable similarities to the world today, most
notably in the incidence of political and social corruption, moral relativ-
ism, and egregious materialism. Socrates bucked the tide of social mores
and openly declared the most important activity human beings can engage in is attention to and concern for one's soul — not care of the body,
or possessions, reputation, and not achievements or accomplishments
— the soul. It is no mere coincidence that the individual in the Western
tradition who epitomizes inquiry, a man who devoted his entire waking

existence to asking questions of anyone and everyone he could, advocated
devotion to the soul. It was Socrates' attitude that says as much about his
reputation for wisdom as anything else. As he tells the story, a friend of his
consulted the oracle at Delphi and was told that "no man is wiser" than
Socrates.[10] Naturally, the friend passed the news along. Socrates could
have responded to the pronouncement in a host of ways: surprise, anxiety,
confusion, disbelief, even smug satisfaction. As an inquisitive person, he
chose not to take the pronouncement at face value. He wanted to know
its *meaning*. Thus the oracle provided the pretext under which Socrates's
destiny unfolded. The wise man of Athens earned his reputation because
he sought wisdom, not because he possessed it.

Socrates's example crystallizes the intimate relationship between addressing the meaning of one's life, concern for the soul, and the art of inquiry. A central question of a meaningful life that extends beyond simple
concern for the self, is "What does life want of me?"[11] This is a persistent
question that one may fruitfully ask many times over the course of a life.
Thus inquiry is a way to live, not a set of skills or a method to use for a
specific project or a limited period of time. Socrates also demonstrated
something else about inquiry that has been taken up by modern depth
psychologists. The theory of the fathomless unconscious, which is the
cornerstone of depth psychology, is an enticement to make the art of inquiry into a lifestyle. Whether the unconscious is defined as personal, or
as personal and collective, matters very little. Either theory gives human
beings a limitless horizon to move toward, a lifetime of questions to ask.
Ultimately whether one's concern is to know the self or to know the world,
in the end they amount to the same thing — a point often misunderstood.
The pursuit of self-knowledge and realization, which Jung called *individuation,* does not begin and end with narcissistic, isolated preoccupation. It
leads to wider consciousness, more intense participation in relationships,
and a larger stake in the world.[12] As the Jungian analyst Edward Whitmont puts it, "one cannot encounter the Self through introversion only.
Human fullness requires the actual meeting with a 'Thou'."[13]

There is little question that a life of inquiry requires sustained courage that bears no resemblance to customary notions of heroic achievement. Rainer Maria Rilke, perhaps moved by the same inspiration that
guided early depth psychologists, advocated such a life. Rilke urged a

young poet he corresponded with to meet the vast and strange reality confronting him by living the questions of his life and having patience with all that is inchoate, unknown and unformed within.

> We must accept our reality as vastly as we possibly can; everything, even the unprecedented, must be possible within it. This is in the end the only kind of courage that is required of us: the courage to face the strangest, most unusual, most inexplicable experiences that can meet us. The fact that people have in this sense been cowardly has done infinite harm to life. Only someone who is ready for everything, who doesn't exclude any experience, even the most incomprehensible, will live the relationship with another person as something alive and will himself sound the depths of his own being.[14]

Rilke goes on to use the metaphor of a room to describe a person who is not capable of facing the inexplicable and who lives a life of fear instead.

> For if we imagine this being of the individual as a larger or smaller room, it is obvious that most people come to know only one corner of their room, one spot near the window, one narrow strip on which they keep walking back and forth.[15]

Poets and depth psychologists revere inquiry because they know it infuses life with worth and meaning. It demands active engagement and not fearful withdrawal into a mere corner of one's existence. This engagement follows the middle way of soul because it pulls people in two directions, upward into the airy reaches of the intellect and downward into the earthy unconscious. Depth psychology's particular contribution is to point out that "knowing thyself" is a messy, confusing, painful business. At no point can inquiry be unyoked from the complex emotional life of the body. The body and the emotions provide some of the best clues for how to proceed, which include knowing which questions are alive and worth pursuing.

PSYCHOLOGICAL INQUIRY

When we speak of inquiry as an art, we are speaking about a kind of inquiry that can rightly be called psychological. Psychological inquiry is not limited to investigating psychological topics. Psychological inquiry is a way of approaching any number of topics, including the arts, literature, humanities, social science, and even natural sciences such as medicine, biology, and physics.

Psychological inquiry into any of these topics is guided by the psyche, which is fathomless, fluid, complex, and speaks in the poetic, associative language of image, metaphor, myth and symbol. This kind of inquiry has two principle characteristics. First, psychological inquiry follows the tradition of respect for and attention to the true complexity of the things of this world. Whereas scientific inquiry tends to reduce observable phenomena to their simplest form, omitting the idiosyncratic in favor of the general, psychological inquiry notes the peculiar and welcomes particularity. Second, the attention to phenomena is not short-lived or easily satisfied because psychological inquiry fundamentally assumes that there is always something more that can be revealed or unfolded. Those engaged in this kind of inquiry seek the deeper meanings of the question, which are often discovered beneath, behind, or just beyond the first layers of understanding. As Marie-Louise von Franz advises, one must remain continually aware of unawareness, keeping "an eye and an ear for the opposite, the other thing."[16] Those who make a habit of psychological inquiry wonder about things, lots of things, a lot of the time. Nothing is taken literally or at face value. Depth psychology's emphasis on the unconscious trains the person to look, then look again. "Who's here?" and "What am I not aware of?" are classic depth psychological questions. In other words, the omnipresent unconscious backdrop that adds layers of depth and mystery to any phenomenon enlivens the process of inquiry. Perhaps it makes inquiry possible.

Let us turn this idea inside out for a moment. Could it be that "What haven't I noticed?" is not merely a question of the inquisitive ego? Perhaps when someone asks "How are these things related?" or "What does that mean?" it is the soul speaking, psyche's logos, psyche's own words. Inquiring may be *the* natural activity of the soul[17] — psyche's way of exploring and revealing itself. Perhaps the soul is inquisitive by nature and human beings who practice the art of inquiry are participants in the soul's own love of knowledge. Phenomenologist Robert Romanyshyn alludes to the psyche's curiosity when he says "I have felt and known for a long time that at our best moments we are always surprised, and that fundamentally we are never the authors of meaning but its agents — agents of, or witness for, soul in its desires for revelation."[18] There is poignant evidence for the soul's desire for revelation in two stories that lie at the heart of the depth psychological tradition: the tale of *Eros and Psyche* and the tragedy of *Oedipus Rex*. In *Eros and Psyche*, Psyche's curiosity drives the story forward and sets her destiny in motion. Without her longing to know Eros her fate would have been quite different. Similarly, in Sophocles's play, Oedipus' unrelenting desire to get to the bottom of his own story — a riveting example of self-examination and its outcome — dramatizes the organic relationship between desire, knowledge, and the soul. Both stories leave the true identity of the seeker, ego or soul, an open question. And perhaps this is just as it should be!

By now our intention should be clear. As depth psychologists we advocate psychological inquiry for the scholar and writer who cherish spontaneity, fluidity, and inclusiveness in the pursuit of a valuable question. We also advocate psychological inquiry as a style of life. We want readers to explore their interests and capacities to the fullest extent and to use their creative work as a means to create themselves. This tradition is an ancient one dating at least back to Socrates who, like modern depth psychologists, placed the soul at the center of human concerns and made inquiry central to his exploration of the soul. The tradition of depth psychology has a unique stake in the practice of inquiry. The next five chapters tell what that stake is and describe the depth psychological contribution to inquiry as an art and as a way of life. We are convinced that the perspective of soul can infuse the practice of inquiry with tremendous depth, meaning, and vitality.

2

HISTORICAL CONTEXTS OF
PSYCHOLOGICAL INQUIRY: A MYTH OF ORIGIN

Chapter 1 introduced the idea that psychological inquiry is not limited to inquiry in the field of psychology. Though psychology is an important area of interest, this book offers a depth psychological perspective on inquiry in many fields including the arts, literature, humanities, social science, and natural sciences when they reach for the deeper meaning of their findings. Therefore this approach is neither esoteric nor without roots. To the contrary, it can be seen as connected to a long-standing tradition of critical philosophy that explores the gaps between theories and actual experiences of living.

Psychological thinking has made essential contributions to developments in philosophy and epistemology since the time of Socrates. These developments have given rise to the vast array of approaches, methods, and methodologies evident today in the field of scholarly inquiry. Therefore even though this is not a book about method, it is valuable to review the more general history of methods and approaches to scholarly and psychological inquiry in order to see how this book, although innovative in many ways, sits in a tradition and has an historical context.

Any attempt to fix a time and place for the beginnings of methodology in scholarly research, at least as a matter of historical fact, will certainly generate justifiable criticism from those who quite rightly might see things otherwise. So we choose the term *myth of origin* rather than history. We offer this one as a valuable way of seeing at least one set of roots or context for understanding the rules human beings have made about understanding.[19] Furthermore, by calling this a myth of origin we acknowledge a mythic sense to these ideas in hopes of rescuing them from being taken literally. This concern is all the more germane in light of the fact that this myth of origin is a Western cultural narrative. Rather than representing some implicit claim that only Westerners are psychological, this narrative presents an opportunity to see these ideas as rooted in an intellectual, historical, and cultural soil. It provides not only a set of assertions but also the wherewithal to criticize them in context.

RATIONALISM, EMPIRICISM, AND THE HUMANISTIC ADVENTURE

Let's begin at a time and place where we can be fairly certain, because there are written records of it, that a profound change took place in the rules by which humans ought to engage the world, and more importantly, engage themselves as beings in the world. The heroic achievements of the European enlightenment brought with them an explosive sense of the capacity of individuals and their communities to influence their own lives through change and innovation. Suddenly everything could be questioned. Certainly the questioning was driven by a commitment to various blends of rationalism and empiricism but this humanistic adventure was, at its heart, a project of critical thinking and liberation from pre-determined, theologically based systems of thought. Dialogues began to emerge that held theological interpretations of the world accountable to lived experience. As a body of scientific knowledge grew throughout the sixteenth and seventeenth centuries, its methods became increasingly committed to mathematics, quantitative inquiry, and proof. There was a convergence of science and philosophy in the academies of Europe that contributed to a vision of human life that could be reduced to units of measurable experience.

Francis Bacon (1561–1626), one of the best and brightest of Elizabethan England, as well as astronomers and mathematicians Galileo Galilei (1564–1642), Johann Kepler (1571–1630), and Isaac Newton (1642–1727) each, in his own way, promoted the idea that scientific inquiry should be based solely on observable, operable, and measurable phenomena. They and others made this claim at a time when emerging technologies provided opportunity for revolutionary insights into the nature of the universe and into the laws of its physical relationships. The result of this splendid florescence of theory, technology, and knowl-

edge was a kind of circular enclosure. Things that could be studied using the new methods and techniques of science became the only real
things — the really important things — because they lent themselves
to such study. The field became limited to the phenomena of the world
that could be observed, reduced, isolated, manipulated, measured, and
controlled. Complexities that might confound and confuse such study
were closed out of the circle. But even within this seemingly unassailable
paradigm there were those who found the world proposed by science to
be too small, too lacking in something essential to humankind.

Blaise Pascal (1623–1662), for example, studied the effects of atmo-
spheric pressure on a column of mercury and invented the barometer.
His work in mathematics was also revolutionary, yielding understandings
of probability and the formulation of the binomial theorem. But Pascal,
like many mathematicians and physicists today, experienced a deepening
spiritual commitment concurrently with the expansion of his scientific
knowledge. Ultimately he came to the point of minimizing the overall
importance of scientific knowledge inasmuch as it was overly dependent
on the blend of sense and reason and could not therefore approach the
deeper questions of existence as effectively as could religion or, if the discipline had existed, psychology.

It is in this intellectual landscape that the French philosopher René
Descartes (1596–1650) divided the phenomena of life into two separate
realms. These two realms are the physical, known through the experience
of the senses, and the spiritual, arrived at solely through human reasoning.
Despite the fact that Descartes's dualistic thesis was primarily inspired by
the somewhat mystical calling of linking human rationality with divine
order, the Cartesian split became an even stronger call to focus human
science on the mechanical and physical dimensions of reality. So what
began as a grand intellectual adventure based on an image of humans as
free to question their reality, eventually produced an image of humans as
mechanistically determined by their sensory experience.

The most significant philosophical shift away from the dominance
of empiricism in human inquiry came with the work of German philosopher, Immanuel Kant (1724–1804). In attempting to revise and renew an
essentially Cartesian view of the dual nature of human experience while

at the same time addressing the critical concerns of a growing number of skeptical thinkers, Kant posited a third kind of knowing. He suggested that innate mental processes guide both human reason and experience. The mind actively participates in the formation of ideas, shaping both experience and reasoning in a kind of reciprocal process. This was a direct challenge to empiricists, who believed that the mind was a passive receptacle of ideas produced by sensations.

Much of Kant's work focused on the act of perception. He convincingly argued that sensory experience of the world is *evoked* by outside physical experience, but it is only made *intelligible* by virtue of innate perceptual forms in the mind. In other words, Kant's view of human rationality grows out of an epistemology that transcends empiricism. This transcendental perspective opens the way for a host of epistemologies based on various forms of subjectivism. If the perceiving mind is actively involved in the construction of reality, it becomes a short step to see that reality is somewhat dependent upon the forms of perception and ultimately upon the character of the perceiving subject. As a result of Kant's influence, the perceiving subject must now be considered in all claims to knowledge. It is no longer easy to hold faith with a pure view of objective reality. This is the beginning of the world wherein the text must be understood in context — at least in the context of its authorship. Investigation does not merely report the truth; it also partly creates the truth, and thus is a deeply interpretive action. Furthermore, in this epistemology knowledge is an activity of understanding rather than of causal explanation.

Though we have credited Kant, the relative subjectivism that he introduced into eighteenth-century European philosophy was foreshadowed at least as early as the ancient Greeks in the tradition of Eclecticism. Relative subjectivism is just one of many ideas that were known, then forgotten, and then remembered as if anew. We will be saying more about the ebb and flow of ideas across time later in this chapter and in subsequent chapters.

EARLY DEVELOPMENTS IN PSYCHOLOGY

As we continue with this myth of origin for scholarly and scientific inquiry it will make good sense to pick up another, coincident narrative. This narrative describes the origins of the field of psychology and the early philosophical commitments that guided psychological method. In the century following Descartes the development of the discipline of psychology in France focused increasingly on the study of sensory processes. Sensation and perception, both subject to observation and measurement in experimental and scientific research designs, became the primary data and ultimately the presumed source of psychological experience. The general term that has been applied to this French psychological school is Sensationalism. To fully understand this idea one might best see it compared with the opposite notion — that being, the supposition of an innate mental capacity or active mind as the basis of the psyche — as we have just described in the discussion on Kant. Mirroring developments in political philosophy during the eighteenth century, French psychology sought to de-emphasize any attachments to the notion of innate mind as the initiator of being. It was too closely linked with traditional theological attitudes, which in turn were too closely linked with monarchical rule. Materialism, with its emphasis on the senses, was a much better fit as a background idea for the nature of existence.

Auguste Comte (1798–1857) in his most famous work, *Cours de philosophie positive* (Course on Positive Philosophy, 1858), used the sensory basis of psychology in an ambitious attempt at a new moral philosophy, a political and social theory, and a methodology based on a practice of observation and description. Comte established a three-part developmental sequence through which one could trace the history of human intelligence and human society. The sequence begins with the theological stage, in which one attempts to understand the world and its human inhabitants in religious context. The second stage is metaphysical, in which one seeks abstract, non-provable explanations for the world. This gives way to the third and final positivist stage, in which one fully explains the world by means of collections of observable facts and the laws that govern their interactions. Comte's elaboration of the sensationalist perspective came to be known as French Positivism.

In a related move Comte posited six basic sciences: mathematics, astronomy, physics, chemistry, physiology or biology, and social physics or sociology. He intentionally omitted psychology, placing the study of the person under physiology and the study of groups under sociology. Comte's bifurcated approach to human psychology reduced the complex phenomena of the psyche into either measurable physical properties or quantifiable observations of social behavior. Those who were temperamentally or philosophically inclined towards complexity had only one alternative: to return to a previous (that is, a more primitive) stage of intellectual inquiry and become mired in some Luddite state of theological or metaphysical ignorance.

This 200-year-old split in the study of human beings has had durable consequences for how research is conducted in the field of psychology down to the present day. In fact, the central calling of the current text begins right in this gap. As researchers with a preference for a depth psychological perspective, we want neither the methods of empirical physical science nor the methods of social science as the only approaches to knowing. Not that they are wrong. They are just not enough. Nevertheless, it is important to note that the social sciences have maintained a strong commitment to the study of complex phenomena. This is reflected in the rich field of qualitative research methodologies. For that reason we are comfortable being cousins in same family and for that reason we continue to explore our common lineage.

Wilhelm Dilthey (1833–1911) is a key figure in our myth of origin for a variety of reasons. His work stands at the generative source of hermeneutics and phenomenology and, in fact, of all interpretive inquiry wherein the primary datum is lived experience. Following the Kantian tradition of positing two kinds of knowledge, Dilthey distinguished between *Naturwissenschaft* and *Geisteswissenschaft*. But Dilthey went on to claim that nature, apart from human consciousness, is unknowable through scientific approaches. What one can study is the *Geisteswissenschaften*. According to Dilthey, this *Geist,* the material of the human sciences, is the only thing truly knowable. Dilthey's claim was quite a reversal. It was, in fact, a whole shift in focus in terms of method and approach to research.

Dilthey's two realms of knowledge seemed to generate two very different experiences of knowing. The *Naturwissenschaften* tended to work at the development of causal explanations or *Erklärung* through the use of general laws. The *Geisteswissenschaften*, on the other hand, produced a kind of depth understanding that Dilthey called *verstehen*.

Verstehen can be best understood in the context of literary hermeneutics. There, *verstehen* implies not just understanding but rather a kind of understanding that is so thoroughly in context that readers come to understand the author's meaning better than the original author by virtue of having a larger view of the author's context. In reading a text, access to two kinds of experience is possible. Readers can become intimately immersed in the author's context at the same time they retain a more distant sensibility. In order to achieve this *better* understanding, however, readers have a formidable task. They must study the world that nurtured the text by investigating history, religion, geography, biography, philosophy, the arts and more — all things that will acquaint readers with the historical-cultural period in which the author lived and wrote. In so doing, readers achieve a broad contextual understanding of the author's work in a way not visible to the author. *Verstehen* thus means not only understanding the meaning of a thing at a technical level but also perceiving the spirit of the author and the age.

The idea behind *verstehen* is not limited to literary hermeneutics. It is an idea about deeper knowing and about knowing that more conforms to the feel of life. And here we find another tremendously important concept first offered by Dilthey — that of *Erlebnis* (lived experience). *Erlebnis* is such a wonderfully paradoxical phrase. It goes to the heart of the flaw in overemphasizing the split between rational and empirical ways of knowing. Actual experience exists more immediately at the level of living than at the level of objective description. Therefore one must strive for ways of knowing that are capable of revealing experiences that begin and remain deeply embedded in social and historical context, and are not reduced beyond the level of recognizable life. Thus, even as Dilthey elaborated the longstanding tradition of articulating the dualistic vision of the psyche, he remembered to reconnect the parts in the actual business of living. The notion of *Erlebnis* — experience not as dissected but as actually lived — became the cornerstone of the new projects of human inquiry about to come into being.

The reweaving move implicit in Dilthey's notion of *Erlebnis* clarifies what has been left out of the story: experience actually lived is lived dialectically. That is, it is lived in the interplay of the various splits we have reviewed — an interplay between mind and body, between spirit and matter, between nature and society and so on.

But it is wrong to imagine that Dilthey somehow invented the idea of *Erlebnis* simply because he invented such a good word for it. The attempt to distinguish lived experience goes back at least two hundred years within the Germanic philosophical context itself, to the work of Baruch Spinoza (1632–1677) who clearly described the actual lived experience of dual consciousness being an ongoing dialectical unity. But for complex reasons, this thread became somewhat lost in the philosophical weavings that followed. Given the right time and place, Dilthey's word *Erlebnis* emerged as a fresh idea. We will be saying a great deal more about the lived experience of a dialectical psyche in the next chapter on the philosophical commitments of depth psychology.

THE BEGINNINGS OF THE SCIENCE OF PSYCHOLOGY

When we talk about the beginnings of psychology it is important to note that lively discussions around the sense of a psychological realm had been taking place in many venues and over many years before the first departments of psychology began appearing in European universities around the turn of the nineteenth century. Of course, the word itself, being Greek in origin, evokes the underlying Greek philosophical concerns: What kind of beings are we? How are we to live? How do we know that, or anything? These questions, and others, had long been seen as psychological as well as philosophical concerns. But in the late 1800s, primarily in Germany, the doctors of modern science began to explore ways to explain the psyche using the same methods that worked so well to explain, control, and manipulate the physical world.

This is not to say that philosophers, theologians, poets, and others abandoned their work on understanding the psyche. Those efforts have continued quite vigorously into the present time. They will surely endure, and perhaps outlive the science of psychology. But the discipline of psychology as something named and recognized by the larger professional world was born within the context of medicine and natural science at the turn of the nineteenth century.

Wilhelm Wundt (1832–1920) stands out as an important figure in determining the course of the new field of psychology. He trained in physiology and medicine and did extensive work with Hermann Helmholtz (1821–1894) at the University of Heidelberg. Helmholtz, also a physiologist, was known for his work on a psychology of perception, which was largely an inductive approach based on physiology. Eventually Wundt left Heidelberg and took a post in inductive philosophy in Zurich. His interest in psychology grew alongside his enthusiasm for physiology and in 1879 he established the first laboratory specifically dedicated to psychological research in Leipzig. Although Wundt's psychology was to become an experimental science of the mind, studied as a natural science akin to biology and physiology, he pushed psychology toward a focus on consciousness rather a focus on elementary process of physiology and devised an analytical approach to its study. The mind would become comprehensible through introspection, a systematic observation and categorization of its contents and its processes.

In a move resonant with that of Auguste Comte some fifty years earlier, Wundt acknowledged that some essential things about humans — for instance how they think, act, and relate to one another — would probably not be studied in what he called "the general psychology." It would be important to understand individuals in a social and cultural context, but only as a separate matter he called the *Volkspsychologie* (folk psychology). Wundt believed that folk psychology properly fell within the domain of another new discipline, anthropology. In Wundt's time this split made functional sense. In fact this was the period in which the fields of anthropology and sociology were growing tremendously. The clear distinction between psychology and social science thus began to take shape. It was a distinction based on the power of method to shape a field. The methods of physiology that natural scientists could successfully apply to the psyche defined the limits of the general psychology. The aspects of the psyche that didn't answer to physiological method were left to others, in this case, the social scientists.

THE SOUL OF PSYCHOLOGY

In recalling that the word psyche originally meant soul, one is obliged to wonder if the business of psychology ought not to include some study of the soul and its way in the world. But science has long since declared the soul off limits, at least in terms of the scientific method. Why? Consider Heraclitus's definition of the soul: "You could not discover the limits of soul, even if you traveled every road to do so, such is the depth of its meaning."[20] This definition presents the science of psychology with two very big problems. First, if the limits of the soul cannot be ascertained, it is, by definition, immeasurable: impossible to calculate or quantify. Second, the direction of soul is downward, toward depth. Science seeks to lift humanity upward towards health and enlightenment, away from symptoms and ignorance. Down is simply the wrong way. Nevertheless, the downward tendency of the psyche is a reality every human knows through living and dying. A logos of the whole psyche must seek ways of understanding this tendency even if it is not measurable.

In pursuit of credibility, early psychologists turned toward physiology and biology. They left this *soul* line of inquiry to those who were already engaged with it and who still pursue it today: philosophers, theologians, and poets. They all are devoted to their own versions of interpretation and have fully engaged the soul aspect of the psyche. At the same time, social scientists have been steady in their commitment to the horizontal dimensions of the psyche. They have helped articulate the qualities of human relationships within and across cultural and societal boundaries. By tracing the philosophical and methodological developments in social science and qualitative research, important thematic parallels that illuminate psychological inquiry at a practical level become apparent.

One particularly psychological thread of philosophy that has also given rise to an important approach to inquiry is phenomenology. It is worthy of special note in the current discussion because phenomenology has taken up several of the key riddles remaining in a reality primarily determined by scientific method. Specifically, phenomenology emphasizes

Dilthey's theme of the *Erlebnis*, or experience as it is lived rather than as it is explained, revealing a layered view of reality. In that layering, explanations of experience are often over-determined in such a way that actual lived experience is obscured and alienated, and must be recovered through particular attention.

Phenomenology explores some Kantian themes as well. Kant's active and participatory view of consciousness is based on the idea of an active and innate personal mind. By taking up the problem of a subject/object split and focusing its study on the intersubjective field, phenomenology begins to describe consciousness as more than personal. It represents relationships of intentionality in which the things of the world want to show themselves at the level of their essence. Consciousness becomes participation with the things of the world, seeking to know them as they are given. Once this step is taken, one must see the world as ensouled — that is, alive with relation and desire.

As a philosophy, phenomenology in the works of Brentano, Dilthey, Husserl, Heidegger, Merleau-Ponty, Gadamer, and many others represents one of the most rigorous and continuous attempts to resolve the puzzles of consciousness. But it is more than a line of philosophical thought. Phenomenology is also a growing body of approaches to and processes of inquiry that require holding a psychological perspective. As a method of inquiry, phenomenology has joined many other qualitative approaches and methods in calling for a return to faithful, rich, and complex descriptions of lived experience.

THE ARTICULATION OF QUALITATIVE METHODS
IN THE TWENTIETH CENTURY

At the same time that natural scientists were refining their methods, becoming reductive in service to precision, the social scientists began a wild century of methodological innovation. To the natural scientist, if the topic could not be studied using the scientific approach it simply would not be studied. To the social scientist, if the topic could not be studied with an existing methodology then it was time to invent another method. This is no small difference. It ultimately leads one away from the fo-

cus on rigidly defined and adhered-to methods and toward a focus on
the moves that keep methods adaptable to increasing needs for complex
understanding.

In Europe and America there has been a dizzying proliferation of
qualitative approaches and methods. Each new method has brought with
it rich possibilities for understanding and its own particular vision of
what it means to be a person in the world. Despite this proliferation,
one can see a central principle unifying the field of qualitative research:
method must serve topic and not the other way round. What researchers
need to study will show itself through the *Erlebnis*, the lived experience. To
respond to the *Erlebnis* requires methodological innovation.

Several authors have attempted to provide some kind of interpretive
map for the developments in qualitative research during the twentieth century. One that seems to have developed some currency, at least in the realm
of social science, has been offered by Denzin and Lincoln. [21] They refer to
"five moments of qualitative research," which we summarize below.

Denzin and Lincoln call the first *moment* or phase of qualitative research the "traditional period" which covers the beginnings of the twentieth century through World War II. This phase included the articulation
of methods of fieldwork by ethnographers like Bronislaw Malinowski and
sociologists including the Chicago School. During this period the emphasis was on the study of what has become known as the exotic other. For
ethnographers this meant people from other cultures — usually thought
of as less developed or more primitive cultures. For sociologists it often
meant studies of marginalized groups and others outside the mainstream
of society. These researchers believed that through the skillful application of methods of observation and the thorough recording of data, they
could produce a more or less objective description of those studied. Time
has shown that some of the philosophical assumptions of this work are
deeply problematic. Among other things, critical theorists have soundly
discredited the notion that a researcher from the outside might be more
able to get at valuable understandings or might have more objectivity. But
it is important to see through such problems to understand how important this engagement with otherness has been in the ongoing critiques of
ethnocentrism and cultural myopia.

The second moment comes roughly at the end of World War II and runs through to the early 1970s. Denzin and Lincoln call this the "modernist phase." This phase was characterized by consistent attempts to stop the methodological wildness by formalizing methods. It was a period wherein methods became linked to particular schools and researchers and were then written into texts in more rigidly codified language. To see this in context one must appreciate the difficulty early qualitative researchers had in gaining credibility within established academia. They were criticized for promoting laziness and a lack of objectivity. The response was to equate rigor with formalism and validity with objectivity.

It seems quite natural in retrospect that the next moment in the history of qualitative research should be a reaction against form for form's sake. Denzin and Lincoln call it the moment of "blurred genres," spanning the 1970s to mid-1980s. All of the various approaches, methods, and processes of qualitative research, as well as their products of data analysis and interpretation, were laid on the table like a smorgasbord. Researchers could pick and choose as the field of study might seem to require. This is the phase in which feminist research began to assert itself. It also saw the articulation of methods that have grown out of related theoretical paradigms such as phenomenology, semiotics, philology, symbolic interactionism, and others.

During the middle of the 1980s a profound critique of the representation of data in social science research began to surface. This gave rise to the fourth moment, the "crisis of representation." Crisis is an apt description to the feel of these times. Critics began to challenge and discredit the subtle but pervasive biases in much of the research being done by established anthropologists and sociologists. The bias was far more extensive than merely the bias of prejudice and ethnocentrism on the part of the researcher. It extended into subtle realms such as language used in interviews, the timing and circumstance of the research, and, perhaps most questionable, the political impetus and disposition of the research. It became clear that research on people and groups has the power to construct reality. It is not merely a benign reporting of a situation. Therefore researchers were representing not only ideas, but also the lives of people, individuals, communities, races, and nations. And this representation was not simply the description of a fixed moment in the passive past, but rather became one determiner of the future. Given this awareness, representation took on a much more significant meaning. It became clear that the time was long overdue for researchers to face legitimate questions about what ideas, and whose, should contribute to that representation.

The impact of the crisis of representation since that time has been to invite a critical perspective into the research process itself. Paradoxically, the value and strength of research is judged partly on its ability to reveal its representational biases and confess its limitations related to perspective. In a way, the crisis of representation in the mid-1980s brought the field of qualitative research back to its philosophical roots. Today, knowledge claims are held accountable to context and to the complexities of both their foundations and their implications. The value of skepticism has re-emerged 2500 years after its articulation in Greek classical thought.

Denzin and Lincoln name this skeptical present, the fifth moment. But rather than suggesting a sweeping invalidation of knowledge claims, this skepticism calls for a faithful consideration of context and for a willingness to see knowledge gained through inquiry as always qualified by time, place, and representation. This is not an anti-intellectual stance purporting that nothing is knowable. Rather it is a challenge to hold knowledge claims in a mutable and conditional way — a key element of psychological inquiry. Depth psychology's particular contribution is to view the mutable nature of knowledge claims as an invitation to continually go deeper in understanding. The protean nature of knowledge simply reflects the protean nature of the psyche, a point we discuss in Chapter 3. Depth psychologists don't begrudge the challenge presented by skepticism, not least of which is potential wounding of the ego that wants to control, dominate, or subjugate areas of knowledge. Depth psychologists also do not belittle the value of any partial knowledge gained. From the depth psychological perspective, knowledge is always partial — it would be hubris to think otherwise — and the unfolding of knowledge is a thing of wonder, not contempt.

The skepticism of the present moment, a deeply psychological moment that reveals the temptation of hubris and offers alternatives, challenges researchers to resist grand narratives and omnipotent theory making. Instead, researchers must begin to see theory making as a matter of narrative: speaking and hearing as essentially interpretive acts or, as we suggest in this chapter, mythical. At the level of methodology, this fifth moment in qualitative research means that formal correctness in the application of method is less important than interpretive transparency. Thus, one ultimately returns to an emphasis on the art of interpretation. The ways and means of knowing are essential to any evaluation of the knowledge itself.

It is no surprise, then, that many researchers have expressed renewed interest in the role of hermeneutics — the art of interpretive knowing — in the new millennium. This has brought the fields of qualitative human inquiry back into dialogue with the humanities, including literature, history, linguistics, philology, semiotics, and studies of mythology and religion. Questions of interpretation and context in these fields have undergone a parallel process of critical review. As it happens, researchers in the humanities have arrived at a similar concern about interpretations and implications in research.

In its fifth moment qualitative research focuses on the art of interpretation, the particularity of context, and reconnects with the original qualitative method: hermeneutics. This reunion of hermeneutics and psychological inquiry is quite fortunate. It points the way toward inquiry that will not be limited by measures of observable behaviors or linear causal laws. It points toward research that can illuminate the lived experience of the psyche in a fuller sense.

The five moments described by Denzin and Lincoln follow the same central theme we have described in our myth of origin for psychological inquiry. It is a theme of methodological innovation and development in continual service to the things that are left out by dominant modes of inquiry. Psychological inquiry has a commitment to find ways to inquire that retain complexity and richness while still requiring devotion to rigorous scholarship and participation in the larger world of the academy. It is clear that work of this kind will require the holding of a tension between the power of tradition and the need for innovation — between the need for a formal method, understood and valued by our colleagues, and the need to move beyond method to recall the things that method forgets.

In Chapters 4 and 5 we will examine the processes of inquiry at the levels of method and methodology, focusing specifically on the particular moves researchers might make when conducting inquiry from a depth psychological perspective. But before we do that it will be important to articulate the philosophical concerns that derive from holding that perspective.

3

PHILOSOPHICAL COMMITMENTS
OF DEPTH PSYCHOLOGY

This central principle of the history of ideas — that all ideas are partial — is perhaps the most important single fact that the human intellect has yet discovered . . . [and] the foundation of wisdom: the mind must be modest. Even if it does not, and probably cannot, know its own limitations, it can be aware that they exist. Does this principle seem obvious? Alas, it is not. One of the dangers of our age, more damaging than ever before, is *total obsession with partial ideas.* [22]

Postmodern critical thought and depth psychology agree on one important and enduring epistemological idea. One's approach to a subject affects what can be seen and learned. At the simplest level the idea is based on the fact of physical existence. Human beings, as embodied flesh-and-blood creatures, can only see something in one way at one time, which means that from moment to moment people operate from *within* a given perspective. The simple expression "now we will turn our attention to . . ." captures this truth. To pay attention to something requires turning towards it — either physically, mentally, or both. And this necessarily means turning away from something else. For this reason, an inquiring person tries always to remember that knowledge, indeed consciousness itself, is always only partial. As much as one might like to be omniscient, it is just not possible. One can reach towards whole knowledge by adopting different perspectives on an issue or question, then use memory, imagination and compassion to weave them into a more comprehensive understanding — and the whole will remain just beyond grasp. But that is no argument against reaching. We believe that it is this gap between reach and grasp that stimulates human creativity, fosters enchantment with the yet-to-be known, and inspires the art of inquiry.

We'll have more to say about the relationship of the part to the whole later in the chapter, but for now we want to assert something important about the partial nature of knowledge and consciousness. We are fully in agreement with L. L. Whyte, who pointed out the very real danger of "total obsession with partial ideas." This obsession is not only an act of hubris; it is profoundly unpsychological.

Twenty-five hundred years ago the Greek philosopher Heraclitus redefined the soul as the dynamic motivating force behind human action and thought, both fathomless and fiery. In Philip Wheelright's commentary on Fragment 45, *The soul has its own principle of growth*, he says this:

> A soul, during the span of time in which it is alive, possesses a real though limited autonomy. In this connection Fr. 45 is significant; for to say that a soul has its own principle of growth is to say that it must be understood not as being pushed into activity from without, but as bestirring itself from within — like a fire rekindling itself from a tiny spark. [23]

A few thousand years later, Freud founded his work on the dynamic nature of the psyche. To be psychological, one adopts the psyche's method and lets perspectives and ideas move freely instead of attempting to make them into outsized, rigid monuments that obliterate other truths. People can begin this practice by becoming aware of their own perspective — or to put it in different language, by understanding the myth they already are living. This is a powerful bit of knowledge that may take months if not years to explore. In the process, people become aware of which sorts of things get their attention and which are overlooked; it reveals how they think and feel about the phenomena that do attract their attention, such as "this is trivial" or "that is unimportant;" finally it suggests the posture of attention they adopt. We have described the two basic postures as the *yin* and *yang* of inquiry. The *yin* of inquiry is patient receptivity while the *yang* of inquiry is an assertive, focused pursuit. These two general postures can be further elaborated to articulate a host of styles. For example the inquiring person can be inclusive, discriminating, precise, penetrating, intimate, distant, hot, cool, insatiable, selective, malleable, reserved, categorical, or impressionable, and each style yields different knowledge and insight; or perhaps they yield knowledge and insight differently. *How* one sees affects *what* one sees.

In guiding readers in the art of inquiry, we want to acknowledge the myth we are living and declare our perspective. Why is this important? Our choice of perspective has affected what we have studied and seen, the methods and moves we have adopted, and the outcome of this work. *The Art of Inquiry* exemplifies the direct and lively relationship between how a person proceeds and what is produced. We believe, and hope to show, that the tradition of depth psychology is uniquely engaging, playful, and inspiring because it is, fundamentally, a philosophy of inquiry. For this reason, what follows is a philosophical exploration of the depth psychological perspective that articulates the commitments it implies. The chapter includes some hints about how best to employ these commitments in work and in life. Simply put, we want readers to know what they are getting into.

Depth psychology is a vast and complex field with a rich history of interconnecting ideas. Attempting to boil these ideas down to a laundry list of core philosophical commitments is a terrific way to spark a fierce and lively debate. That's fine. In fact, engaging in the debate to clarify these ideas is essential. Each person needs to test them through an engagement with his or her feeling function, the deliberate and discriminating process by which someone knows their deepest values. Without their own ideas, people too easily become victims of someone else's epistemology and remain estranged from their own. Without an adequate epistemology, people cannot engage in authentic psychological inquiry because they won't know how to learn. Without a good and useful idea of how to learn, they will not be capable of enlisting the attention, support, and wisdom of an indefatigable teacher, the psyche. To paraphrase an ancient adage, the student must be ready for the teacher to appear.

In the spirit of Hermes, that mercurial power who loves the fiery exchange of words, and his orderly brother Apollo, who is rather fond of laundry lists, herewith are eight philosophical commitments of depth psychology that are critical to the art of inquiry:

□ The psyche is real

□ The psyche is a perspective

□ The psyche is both personal and more than personal

□ The psyche is fluid and protean

□ The psyche is symptomatic

□ The psyche is multiple and relational

□ The psyche is complex and contradictory

□ The psyche is dialectical

As we describe each of these commitments in detail, we invite you to take the ideas psychologically. That is, please read, absorb, engage, reflect, challenge, feel, imagine, think, and critique. Then use the ideas to think of yourself as a soul embarking on the odyssey of psychological inquiry, in lively dialogue with the psyche.

COMMITMENT I: THE PSYCHE IS REAL

All depth psychologists believe in the reality of the unconscious and take the whole psyche, which includes both consciousness and the unconscious, as their primary datum. This distinguishes *depth* psychology from other approaches such as cognitive, behavioral, experimental, and social psychology. For instance, three prominent authors and social psychologists, Howard Gardner, Mihaly Csikszentmihalyi, and William Damon, published a book entitled *Good Work* in which they define themselves as "social scientists of the mind." This is a fine description of a particular style of psychology. In fact, it alludes to the kind of psychology familiar to most people, one that pays attention to human beliefs and behavior in a social context. A depth psychologist might begin examining a person's belief or behavior, but only as a trapdoor into the more remote recesses of the individual psyche and to the wealth of connections between the individual soul and other souls which situate and nourish it. Depth psychology, as its name implies, draws one beneath the surfaces of thought, word, and action to the inclinations and impulses of the soul they are rooted in.

The first generation of depth psychologists, Sigmund Freud (1856–1939), Alfred Adler (1870–1937), and C. G. Jung (1875–1961), focused on the unconscious but did not discover it. For example, ancient Greeks believed in the healing power of dreams and wondered about their mysterious source, as do members of other indigenous cultures around the world from Africa to Australia to the Americas. Just prior to Freud, European philosophers and artists of the eighteenth and nineteenth centuries looked to the unconscious as the ground of individuality and the source of poetic inspiration. In perhaps the most dramatic instance, Samuel Taylor Coleridge reportedly dreamt the entire text of his poem *Kubla Kahn* and, upon awakening, wrote most of it down. Freud's pioneering contribution to human knowledge of the unconscious lay in using the emerging tools of scientific analysis to observe mental processes and develop a systematic theory of the structure and dynamics of the psyche. Freud maintained that no thought, feeling, inspiration, memory, or action occurred randomly. Only a theory of an unconscious as a counterpart to ego consciousness could explain the meaning and purpose of supposedly irrational behavior. Freud's work was startling, provocative, and beautifully articulated, and he made the language of depth psychology part of everyday lexicon. Today, many people who have never read a word of Freud's work in translation freely use terms such as *ego*, *id*, *superego*, *repression*, *libido*, and the *unconscious*.

Freud's followers, particularly Jung and Adler, had significant and acrimonious theoretical disagreements with Freud. Ultimately each man founded his own school of thought that attracted its particular set of philosophical adherents and professional analysts. Though these three "fathers of depth psychology" developed different ways of perceiving and working with the unconscious, a heretofore neglected aspect of the psyche, they nonetheless agreed that it was the primary object of their interest and research. Not one of them doubted that the psyche was real. In other words, at a time when positivism had established its intellectual hegemony throughout the Western world, Freud, Adler, and Jung withstood the scorn and contempt of their more conventional peers to explore the unconscious. They could not probe the unconscious directly in the same way they would conduct a physical examination. But it could be detected through its effect, and this they proceeded to study with all the rigor of any determined scientist.

As an aside, the exploration of the unconscious was coterminous with another similar development in the physical sciences. In the first part of the twentieth century, Albert Einstein began to search for a theory that would integrate all known discoveries about the physical world. He was virtually alone at the time, but within fifty years many more physicists, though not all, would embrace Einstein's vision. Seeking one neat "theory of everything" has been described as the Holy Grail of physics, a suggestive metaphor that hints at the passionate and mysterious nature of this quest. In physics, a field refers to an area under the influence of an invisible force that is known through its visible effect on the phenomenal world. Gravitational (electromagnetic) fields exemplify this. An invisible field that produces visible effects is a cogent description of the unconscious, the evidence for which also is inferential. Depth psychologists infer the existence of the invisible unconscious by seeing its visible effect in dreams, in symptoms, and in psychopathology. The simultaneous investigations for a unified field theory in physics and for a personal and transpersonal unconscious in depth psychology are an interesting bit of synchronicity. Jung observed that the conjunction of these two lines of inquiry in two separate human disciplines is suggestive. Though their relationship to one another is "extremely hypothetical" it is nonetheless worth entertaining. "Sooner or later," Jung said, "nuclear physics and the psychology of the unconscious will draw closer together as both of them, independently of one another and from opposite directions . . . push forward into transcendental territory." [24]

Freud fully understood the difficult task of making psychoanalysis a legitimate area of medical research and a science in its own right. In a paper on the unconscious that he published at the end of 1915, he replied to critics that "our assumption of the unconscious is necessary and legitimate, and that we possess numerous proofs of its existence." [25] These proofs included the substantial gaps in conscious mental functioning of healthy people such as slips of the tongue, (now known colloquially as "Freudian slips"), behavioral anomalies, and dreams.

Inferring the existence of the unconscious utilized a valid scientific principle, induction, which means to arrive at a generalized conclusion (or theory) based on observation of particular instances. Freud took great pains to defend his right as a scientist to develop a theory of the unconscious in this way. Since theoretical constructs are the means by which any science advances itself, why should psychoanalysis as the scientific exploration of the unconscious be any different? Freud argued that the method of psychoanalytical research was identical with other research sciences. It begins with "describing phenomena" and then proceeds "to group, classify, and correlate them." Like other sciences, the phenomena under psychoanalytic scrutiny suggested the application of "certain abstract ideas to the material in hand, ideas derived from somewhere or other but certainly not from the new observations alone. Such ideas — which later become the basic concepts of the science — are still more indispensable as the material is further worked over." Moreover, psychoanalytical ideas are continually justified by "having significant relations to the empirical material." [26] The unconscious was just such an idea.

Freud's arguments are stylistically brilliant and logically persuasive. Yet for all his considerable effort, depth psychologists since Freud have felt the need to take up the same gauntlet. Positivism, the belief in the validity *only* in what can be seen and measured, is alive and well 100 years after Freud. For example, in one of the most dramatic moments in the Houston interviews with C. G. Jung filmed in the 1950s, he *insisted* that the psyche is real. Like Freud, this was the core tenet of Jung's approach to depth psychology. However, rather than speak of the unconscious as a scientifically valid theoretical construct, Jung more often alluded to it as a fundamental experience of the human condition. Jung tended to emphasize belief in the unconscious that was grounded in direct experience of psychic phenomena, something akin to a belief in god grounded in direct experience of the sacred. This gave Jung's philosophical position and his psychological method a very different flavor than that of Freudian psychoanalysis. It might loosely be called spiritual as opposed to Freud's emphasis on the scientific. However, this distinction must not be distorted through overemphasis. The two men had more in common than not. They were medical doctors who, by temperament and training, paid minute attention to the phenomena their patients presented in the clinical setting.

Freud looked for the origin of current illness in the patient's past, emphasizing a retrospective look at life lived thus far. He stated that "analytic experience has convinced us of the complete truth of the assertion so often to be heard that the child is psychologically father to the adult and that the events of his first years are of paramount importance for his whole later life."[27] The period of childhood was key, Freud argued, because it is the short, intense period of time when the ego is molded by internal demands and external influences to produce a functioning member of society. "In the space of a few years the little primitive creature must turn into a civilized human being; he must pass through an immensely long stretch of human cultural development in an almost uncannily abbreviated form."[28] The prohibitions and punishments the child encountered inevitably led to wounding, which years later showed up in the suffering adults who came to Freud for psychoanalytic help. His aim was to alleviate this suffering and give the ego greater freedom and control.

Like Freud, Jung also wanted his patients to develop the ego strength needed to respond to life with more freedom. Jung's emphasis, however, was on developing the relational capacity of the ego. A strong ego is an ego capable of relating to the Self, the *imago dei* (image of God) which is the archetype of wholeness and contains the seeds of future life. In one of Jung's letters, he uses the metaphors of straw and stone to describe this kind of ego strength:

> God wants to be born in the flame of man's consciousness, leaping ever higher. And what if this has no roots in the earth? If it is not a house of stone where the fire of God can dwell, but a wretched straw hut that flares up and vanishes? Could God then be born? One must be able to suffer God. That is the supreme task for the carrier of ideas. He must be the advocate of the earth.[29]

Relationship with the Self is not for the sole benefit of the individual person. Rather it is the way that the psyche, which is more than personal, expresses *its* creativity and comes to know *itself*. "There is no other way in which [the psyche] could express itself except through the individual human being."[30] Only the substantial person, the true individual who is strong enough to suffer the Self without being overwhelmed, can become

a carrier of ideas and an advocate of the earth. This role demands ego sta-
bility, intellectual dedication, and psychological wisdom — a formidable
combination of aptitudes.

Jung found that the unconscious offers ego consciousness insight
into the past and also leads individuals and communities toward their
future. It is continually producing images to assist patients with the essential task of becoming whole over the course of their lives. Though the
person never achieves wholeness, it is possible to move toward it by responding thoughtfully and sensitively to the clues the psyche offers. Jung
had few illusions about the challenges inherent in living with the reality
of the whole psyche. There are many reasons for ignoring or forgetting
the existence of the unconscious in particular. Much of the time the ego
prefers to see itself as coterminous with the entire psyche rather than as
one small part of it. Often, the contents of the unconscious that do rise
to the surface of awareness are disturbing and confusing; unwelcome her-
alds of things most people would rather ignore. Living with the reality of
the psyche, which requires attention to such unconscious stirrings, takes
time and effort. But ignoring the unconscious in any given moment does
not negate its reality or effects. As Andrew Stevens says, the unconscious
"exists as a perpetual companion to consciousness; its utterances in words
and symbolic images proceed ceaselessly below the threshold of everyday awareness."[31] When one acknowledges the reality of the psyche, this
perpetual companion of ego consciousness makes itself known. It is not
simple, as we have said, but it does ensure that one's life and work will be
deeply creative and full of meaning.

COMMITMENT 2: THE PSYCHE IS A PERSPECTIVE

In Jung's essay "Instincts and the unconscious," he put forward the idea
that archetypes are "modes of apprehension."[32] That is, they aren't simply manifestations of psyche, they are the way the person sees and un-
derstands. Anyone who has been caught in a complex — the tangible
manifestation of an archetype — can readily understand this. Writers
use colors and symbols to describe the experience, for instance, "she saw
red" as a description of someone who is enraged. The emotion of rage
symbolically *colors* everything that the enraged person sees. To speak in

archetypal terms, one might describe that person as possessed by Kali, the Hindu goddess of creativity and destruction, or refer to it as a visitation from Ares, the hotheaded Greek god of war.

James Hillman takes Jung's idea that archetypes are modes of apprehension and expands it. In the preface to his book *Revisioning Psychology*, Hillman describes the psyche (soul) as an archetype and, therefore, as a way of seeing. "By soul I mean . . . a perspective rather than a substance, a viewpoint toward things rather than a thing itself." [33] Later in the book he argues that soul is not a subject, a body of knowledge that one acquires, but the way one acquires knowledge about anything at all. Psyche is an epistemology: "The soul is less an object of knowledge than it is a way of knowing the object, a way of knowing knowledge itself." [34]

Jung was not the first depth psychologist to view psychology as a field of knowledge and to use psychology as a critical perspective on other subjects, such as literature or art. Some of Freud's most memorable writings are his analyses of culture, religion, and history, in which he applies the principles of psychoanalysis and interprets the deep meaning of widely ranging subject matter for his readers. Freud's impact on culture was recently acknowledged in an exhibition of his works, selected from the Library of Congress's collection of more than 112 million diverse items. James H. Billington, the Librarian of Congress, stated that "while controversy still abounds in medical, literary, and academic circles over Sigmund Freud and his work . . . few would disagree that his chief legacy — the psychoanalytic movement — has had an enormous impact on Western culture in the twentieth century." [35] Freud's interpretations of culture are sometimes startling and always provocative. At the very least, works like *Totem and Taboo*, *Civilization and its Discontents*, and *The Future of an Illusion* substantiate the idea that the depth psychological perspective offers valuable insight not revealed by other ways of thinking and thus augments human understanding and knowledge.

In the spirit of Freud's wide-ranging application of psychoanalysis to culture, depth psychologists including Freudians and Jungians continued to move the new discipline inexorably beyond the bounds of clinical praxis. Over the course of the twentieth century, depth psychology became "a form of thought, an approach to human experience, that has become constitutive of our culture and pervades the way we have come to experience ourselves and our minds." [36] One of Jung's many contributions was to describe psychology as an ontology, a way of being, and to lay the groundwork for the archetypes as ways of knowing. Hillman, in his development of archetypal psychology, expanded Jung's notion that psychology is an epistemology by naming psyche as an archetype, thereby claiming soul as a perspective. This perspective, he says, is reflective, deep, and metaphorical. It "makes differences between ourselves and everything that happens," which invites reflection.[37] Opening this gap between the self and the stuff of life permits one to learn about both self and world. The perspective of psyche, in other words, provides the opportunity to develop a richer, deeper, and more imaginative mind simply by paying attention. As Jung would say, people become distinct personalities by virtue of the fact that they enter into a psychological relationship with every aspect of life — and with life itself.

Hillman describes precisely what he means by the soul perspective. It is the deepening of events into experiences, it has a special relationship with death, and it refers to a symbolic or metaphorical approach to life. Let's discuss each of these in greater detail.[38]

First, "soul refers to the deepening of events into experiences." [39] This is where attention is paramount. The soul perspective is an invitation to pause and attend, to go beneath the glittering, sometimes brittle surfaces of hectic life to allow a simple, fleeting event to take root. This metaphor suggests substance and slow growth and darkness and fertility. An experience matters. It is something that is felt at the deepest levels of being. The presence of feeling, arousal, and meaning — all indications that eros is stirring — is the hallmark of a soul experience. That is why an experience is always more psychological than a mere event.

Second, Hillman argues, the soul perspective which transforms a fleeting event into a significant experience derives from the soul's "special relation with death." [40] This relationship between the soul and death has a long history. "Greek poetic tradition from Homer through Plato conceived of the psyche primarily in terms of death, that is, in relation with the underworld or the afterlife." Death, in this case, is more symbolic than literal. It refers to "the point of view 'beyond' and 'below' life's concerns." [41] In its kinship with death, the perspective of psyche pulls the person below the surface into the depths to look at things another way. This pull towards death is a specific antidote for the hectic pace of modern life that celebrates endless consumption of things, people and events. The perspective of psyche exposes the cherished illusion "that growth is but an additive process requiring neither sacrifice nor death. The soul favors the death experience to usher in change." [42]

Finally, Hillman says that the soul perspective refers to "the imaginative possibilities in our natures, the experiencing through reflective speculation, dream, image, and fantasy — that mode, which recognizes all realities as primarily symbolic or metaphorical." [43] When people pause to speculate on the meaning of a particular event, they see *beyond* its simple presentation to acknowledge that there is more here than meets the eye. They open up to the richness of the psyche and multiply possibilities rather than close down and limit possibilities. In other words, adopting the soul perspective trains people to imagine the invisible whole, the matrix or field that contains the visible part. David Abram, who writes as a magician and a phenomenologist, says that the imagination

> is from the first an attribute of the senses themselves; imagination is not a separate mental faculty (as we so often assume) but is rather the way the senses themselves have of throwing themselves beyond what is immediately given, in order to make tentative contact with the other sides of things that we do not sense directly, with the hidden or invisible aspects of the sensible. And yet such sensory anticipations and projections are not arbitrary; they regularly respond to suggestions offered by the sensible itself. [44]

Abram places provocative emphasis on the responsive nature of imagination. He redefines imagination as intense participation with the sensible world instead of disengagement from it. [45] Psychologizing is *seeing through* a phenomenon to what is behind, beneath, or on the other side of it. In the following passage, Hillman describes it as a style of attention that requires participation, curiosity, and above all flexibility.

Changes of physical position and attitude can be metaphors for seeing through. To psychologize we need to get closer or even to "backoff" for a different perspective or to look at things from a different angle. Other motifs are: turning lights on or off, entering, descending, climbing up or fleeing to gain distance, translating, reading or speaking another tongue, eyes and optical instruments, being in another land or another period of history, becoming insane or sick or drunk — all of which are concrete images for shifting one's attitude to events, scenes, persons. [46]

The flexibility needed to shift perspective points the way towards the one thing that kills psychological inquiry: rigidity. People need to remain alert to any hints of dogmatism in their attitude without sacrificing the dedication and discipline necessary to the quest for knowledge. The specific motifs Hillman mentions — entering, descending, climbing up or fleeing to gain distance — are *not* just bodily metaphors for intellectual moves. The flexibility of perspective required in psychological inquiry often is a matter of actual physical movement.

As Robert Romanyshyn explains, "the most ordinary but also the most primary fact about a person and his or her body is that the person *is* his or her body," which means every human action, from pace to posture to gesture, is indicative of one's character, history, and desire. [47] There exists an intimate connection between fleshy body and fluid perspective. Learning is rooted in lived experience, even when its full consummation urges the person toward the heights and breadth of intellectual understanding. People know what they know through sensation, intuition and imagination working in concert with reason.

One obligation that arises in adopting psyche as a perspective is continual self-awareness, which might include asking some of the following questions: "What is my attitude now, open, receptive, stubborn, dogmatic?" "Am I trying to be right or am I willing to be surprised or challenged?" Other questions are "What am I not seeing?" and "Who am I not hearing?" Such self-awareness, though relatively simple, is nonetheless demanding. Another obligation is to view any sort of inquiry as a dialogue between the worker and everything seeking participation in the work. The question is what kind of dialogue and with whom? According to convention, dialogue is conversation with other human beings. This limits dialogue to a human enterprise and alienates humanity from the rest of the animated world and the *anima mundi*. For people who adopt psyche as a perspective, dialogue can and does include the figures who show up in dreams, fantasies, and artwork as well as the natural and man-made things of the world. They are considered psychically real and their presence is assumed to be meaningful rather than random or accidental. The perspective of psyche fosters a particularly rich way of relating to the world. The person who thrives is someone who is willing to be informed, holding the posture of a continual apprentice to life and all that it has to teach.

COMMITMENT 3: THE PSYCHE IS PERSONAL
AND MORE THAN PERSONAL

One of the most significant of Freud's many contributions to depth psychology was his decision to take his patient's symptoms seriously even in the absence of a physiological cause. Rather than dismiss these individuals as "mere hysterics," Freud sought another explanation for their symptoms. He moved beyond a strict consideration of the biological origin (etiology) of the neuroses and began to address what is known in eastern wisdom traditions as the subtle body. In other words, Freud recognized that human beings were bodies *and* souls and that either one of them or both could be wounded. For Freud, the psyche was bounded by and contained within *human* bodies and never found elsewhere. To address soul issues, Freud treated individuals and their personal history, and did not venture far beyond the family of origin.

The emphasis on curing patients is a significant feature of Freudian psychology and many other traditional forms of clinical work. The therapist in partnership with the patient attempts to detect and solve psychological problems; in other words to effect, with some partial measure of success, a cure. Freud was very modest in his goal. He hoped only to transform neurotic misery into common unhappiness. He asserted that at this stage in human history no more is possible because no one can entirely escape the modern neurotic condition. Neurosis, Freud argued in *Civilization and its Discontents*, is a byproduct of the civilizing process. Social existence per se — and human beings can only live socially — is both frustrating and fulfilling for individuals.

In his *Outline of Psycho-Analysis* Freud succinctly described the goal and the process of psychoanalytic treatment:

> The analytic physician and the patient's weakened ego, basing themselves on the real external world, have to band themselves together into a party against the enemies, the instinctual demands of the id and the conscientious demands of the super-ego. We form a pact with each other ... Our knowledge is to make up for his ignorance and to give his ego back its mastery over lost provinces of his mental life. This pact constitutes the analytic situation. [48]

The Freudian approach envisions the individual psyche as an unrelenting battleground of contending forces. In Freud's 1923 essay *The Ego and the Id*, which is considered the definitive articulation of his mature theory, Freud uses several metaphors to suggest this. One of the ego's most important jobs is to try to defend against the murderous tendencies of the id and the reproaches of the superego; to find some way to satisfy their conflicting desires and, at the same time, mediate between these internal demands and external reality. It is a never-ending task requiring the diplomacy of a statesman and the perseverance of Sisyphus. The analyst is the ego's only ally, and analysis is effective in part because the analyst never underestimates the relentlessly unstable state of affairs.

Three key assumptions are embedded in this psychoanalytic model. The first assumption is that the psyche to be addressed is an individual one (though the psyche does come into being dialectically in relationship to primary others). Second, the individual psyche suffers from its own divisions and longs for healing. Third, the beneficiary of the attention is the individual person, which has tended to mean the individual ego and not the soul. The central challenge in ego-oriented psychotherapy is, "How can we (analyst and patient) get rid of this symptom (i.e., this manifestation of the psyche) so that I (the patient) feel better?" As Hillman points out, such an attitude insists that "all my subjectivity and all my interiority must literally be mine, in ownership of my conscious ego-personality. At best we have souls; but no one says we are souls." In fact, "conventional psychology rarely even uses the word soul: a person is referred to as a self or an ego."[49] Particularly from the perspective of ego psychology, which is the broadest therapeutic tradition in America to grow directly out of psychoanalysis, concern for the soul is nearly absent.[50]

Jung agreed with Freud on the extensive influence of the unconscious. Patients' ideas or imaginations of themselves are just as real as the breathing, moving, thinking, and feeling person that physically exists. Moreover, the consequences are just as real. An injured idea of the self can be as limiting as an injured limb. It is just at this point, however, that Jung made a radical departure from Freud. He found evidence for a transpersonal and suprahuman psyche in addition to the individual psyche. In his early work, Jung called this the collective unconscious. Later, in his 1934 essay *The Development of the Personality,* Jung began referring to this transpersonal, collective unconscious as the *objective psyche.*

To describe the boundless and containing quality of the objective psyche, Jung borrowed the Latin phrase *unus mundus,* which literally translates to "one world." He stated that "Psyche and matter exist in one and the same world, and each partakes of the other.... Synchronistic [events] point to a profound harmony between all forms of existence."[51] For Jung, the phrase "all forms of existence" includes what is conventionally considered to be real — *matter* that one can touch, see, taste, smell, hear and above all measure — and also what is conventionally considered imaginary or a fantasy, which includes *nonmaterial* images, sensations, and intuitions. A thorough and meaningful approach to the psyche needs to address what is and what is not bounded by the individual human body.

Jung believed that all forms of life have a telos, which is the urge to become a distinct and complete individual. This is the creative drive, which he called *individuation.* As human beings individuate, consciousness of the self increases simultaneously with consciousness of what is not self. The process of differentiating self from other fosters genuine relationship; without differentiation no relationship is possible. Individuation requires a lifelong relationship with the unconscious that begins with attention to the personal psyche but does not end there. Eventually it includes adopting a receptive attitude to everything, which produces a refined awareness of the individual self as a psychic being in relationship with the more-than-personal psyche. In part because the world is a plenitude of phenomena, the process of individuation inevitably "leads to more intense and broader collective relationships and not to isolation."[52] The individuating person expands outward, actively relating to the more-than-personal psyche rather than contracting into narrow self-absorbed preoccupation with the personal psyche. Hillman sums it up nicely: "The self-knowledge that depth psychology offers is not enough if the depths of the world soul are neglected. A self-knowledge that rests within a cosmology which declares the mineral, vegetable, and animal world beyond the human person to be impersonal and inanimate is not only inadequate. It is also delusional."[53]

For people deeply engaged in the art of inquiry, Jung's more inclusive definition of the psyche is fruitful. Among other things, it suggests that any work a person undertakes has as much psychic reality as the worker. It is an active, autonomous participant in its own development, with legitimate demands and desires, on the path of its own individuation. Though one may wish to control the creative process, it is only possible to guide its course. A more psychological approach is to treat the work as an autonomous partner by entering into a lively, dialectical relationship with it, fully prepared for the unexpected and the synchronistic. In the realm of the psyche, all authors are co-authors.

Perhaps a helpful way to view the art of inquiry is to use the metaphor of a journey. One is engaged in an odyssey, poised between the worlds of death and life, and implicated in their rich fusion. Mythologist and cultural anthropologist Karl Kerényi offers a beautiful description of what this feels like in the midst of the experience.

> The situation of the journeyer is defined by movement, fluctuation ... The journeyer is at home while underway, at home on the road itself, the road being understood not as a connection between two definite points on the earth's surface, but as a particular world ... Being open to everywhere is part of [the road's] nature. Nevertheless, they form a world in its own right, a middle domain, where a person has access to everything. He who moves about familiarly in this world-of-the-road has Hermes for his God.[54]

It is no coincidence that the god of journeys is Hermes, the archetypal communicator and guide of souls. What livelier companion could there be on such an odyssey?

COMMITMENT 4: THE PSYCHE IS FLUID AND PROTEAN

Freud had one primary concern as he developed psychoanalysis into a science and a therapeutic practice: to pay close attention to the fluctuating contents of the conscious mind, or ego, and its dynamic relationship to the unconscious. His theory of psychodynamics, the idea that the psyche is fluid, is expressed in three of Freud's core ideas. The first idea is that the structures of the psyche, ego, id and superego, dynamically evolve out of one another in early life and thereafter their interrelationship remains a struggle for balance and control. The second idea is that each of the human drives or instincts is a flow of energy, which Freud called libido, and that this flow changes in intensity and can be redirected from one object to another. And the third idea is that the contents of ego consciousness are always changing, which reflects the dynamic interrelationship between ego, id, and superego.

Freud's map of the psyche underwent significant revision over the course of his long professional career, as did many of his theories. They have been further modified, extended, challenged, and transformed since his death in 1939. In his mature theory, Freud showed that "the mental apparatus" of an individual consists of "three realms or provinces," namely the id, the ego, and the superego.[55] These three realms owe their genesis to the dynamic nature of the psyche. Ego arises out of id as a response to reality and to fulfill its task of self-preservation. The ego then distils more energy from the id to form the super-ego, an internal representation of the civilizing influence of external authority figures. Once these structures are formed in early childhood, they remain in dynamic relationship to one another and influence the individual's life in visible and invisible ways. The id continues to express the basic drives in dreams, fantasies, and symptoms. The superego continues to reinforce the ego ideal and enforce an acceptable standard of behavior. The ego continues to be responsible for managing the continual flux of competing demands from the id and the superego while simultaneously attempting to adapt itself to reality. Freud described the ego's task of self-preservation as "economic" to emphasize the attributes of exchange and competition between the three structures of the psyche.

Libido, or energy, moves among these three structures of the psyche, id, ego, and superego. An important characteristic of libido is the ease with which it can move from one object to another. Freud distinguished two aspects of the basic human drives: physical drives (needs) and mental drives (wishes). In his late theory, he concluded that there were just two categories of basic drives: the sexual or erotic drive and the death drive. The needs and wishes the individual attempts to satisfy, especially those arising out of the sexual (erotic) drive, are "remarkable for their plasticity." [56] Thus a core tenet of Freudian depth psychotherapy is that individuals can satisfy their needs or wishes in a great number of different ways. The plasticity of the psyche is one of the means by which individuals express their uniqueness. Sculptors channel some of their libido into creating three-dimensional art, writers channel their libido onto the page, parents channel their libido into raising children, and entrepreneurs channel theirs into starting a company. Libido or energy that is stuck, failing to behave like energy, signals psychic distress. The word "fixated" describes this neurotic condition, and reinforces the core idea that a healthy psyche is a fluid psyche.

The fluidity of the psyche is also evident in the way contents of consciousness change. As Freud put it, "consciousness is in general a highly fugitive state. What is conscious is conscious only for a moment." [57] One minute the person may remember something important or necessary and the next moment it may slip back into the unconscious. The fugitive nature of consciousness is one of the most consistently intriguing and occasionally disturbing aspects of the psyche. For better or for worse, the psyche is never in stasis. If people expend no energy keeping the thought or memory from consciousness, then they can recall it again easily enough. In fact, people characteristically produce an assortment of thoughts, images, memories, wishes and fantasies in a given period of waking life, nor does the flow stop when they are asleep. This fact is the most convincing evidence of the psyche's fluidity.

Jung agreed with Freud that the psyche is fluid, though his emphasis was slightly different. He did not describe the psyche as a battleground of contending forces. Instead, Jung adapted the symbol system of alchemy — the esoteric medieval art and precursor to modern chemistry — to speak about the fluid and dynamic nature of psychological processes. In alchemy, the adept worked material that was continually undergoing transformation. Each stage of the process, such as *separatio* (cutting, separating), *solutio* (dissolving), *coagulatio* (solidifying), and *sublimatio* (evaporating), described a substance in movement. Another metaphor we like for the fluid psyche, homier than alchemy, is cooking. Imagine making tonight's dinner, beginning with raw food and ending up with a cooked meal. The psyche works in very much the same way; continually in movement like any other organic substance, one stage of a process organically leading to another.

Jung also believed the fluid psyche is a self-regulating system like the body. It attempts to maintain equilibrium through a natural dialectic. "Every process that goes too far immediately and inevitably calls forth compensations, and without these there would be neither a normal metabolism nor a normal psyche." On this basis, Jung argued that "we can take the theory of compensation as a basic law of psychic behavior."[58] The compensatory nature of the psyche was reflected in Jung's theory of the archetypes as basic patterns or dynamic processes that constitute individual identity. For instance, the ego, which is the conscious personality, is compensated by the shadow, which behaves something like an unconscious personality. The contrasexual archetypes, anima and animus, provide a counterbalance for the individual's biological gender. In a man, the anima or archetypal feminine compensates for his maleness. In a woman, the animus or archetypal masculine compensates for her femaleness. Archetypal psychology, articulated by James Hillman, points out that a person of either gender may discover both an anima and an animus in the unconscious. The psyche is even more polytheistic, Hillman argues, than classical Jungian theory suggests.

While the basic archetypes such as ego, persona, shadow, anima, and animus develop over time and remain more or less present throughout a person's life, some archetypes manifest unexpectedly and spontaneously.

Their sudden presence illustrates the fluid nature of the psyche. It is possible to detect not only their presence but also their purpose and meaning as well. For instance, the image of Hecate or Artemis may emerge from the unconscious when a person's psyche needs more solitude and unrelatedness. "The archetype is not only an 'elementary thought' but also an elementary poetical image and fantasy, and an elementary emotion, and even an elementary impulse towards some typical action." Jungian psychology embellished the classical Greek archetype as pure Form or Ideal by adding to it "a whole sub-structure of feeling, emotion, fantasy, and action." [59] One does not merely perceive the archetype in an abstract, disembodied manner. One is often fascinated, compelled, or gripped by the archetype.

Jungian scholar Andrew Samuels considers the meaningful relationship between the turning points in someone's life and the appearance of archetypes.

> Because archetypal layers of the psyche are, in some sense, fundamental, they tend to produce images and situations which have a tremendous impact on the individual, gripping him and holding him in a grip, often, but not always, with an accompanying feeling of mystery and awe; he will be unable to remain unaffected. We can speculate that turning points in a person's life are in many cases workings out of archetypal activity. [60]

People who are about to undertake a creative work or who are entering a new stage in life often find an archetypal image, idea, or fantasy germinating in their psyche. Or they may feel themselves drawn to a place, a community, or an issue. By keeping the libido theory in mind, one can notice when a portion of energy is channeling itself in the new direction. This alerts the person to the fact that it is becoming erotic in the largest sense, and there is fuel for the creative fire.

On the other hand, one may feel that the libido is stopped, stuck, or it has drained away or moved on to another interest. How might one respond to this shift in eros? It's easy to become frustrated and despondent; there may well be a real loss involved here that requires a time of grieving. Instead of putting up a fight, this might be a good time to adopt the *yin* posture of inquiry and follow the movements of eros just exactly as they are. As Hillman notes, eros has many ways of expressing itself:

> Rejection, impotence and frigidity may also be eros expressions, part of the daimon's 'nay'. . . . Eros need not be fought, controlled, or transformed into something nobler. *Its goal is always, in any case, psyche.* We are obliged to trust eros and its goal. Can anyone live authentically unless he believes and trusts in the basic meaningfulness and rightness of the movements of his love?[61]

Following the flow of eros is one way to acknowledge the fluid psyche. Allowing images and objects to come forward and express themselves — and also to fade back into unconsciousness where they gestate in the dark — supports the creative process and the creative person in a deeply revitalizing and transformative process.

COMMITMENT 5: THE PSYCHE IS SYMPTOMATIC

Freud and Jung paid particular attention to the individual and unique manifestations of the psyche, the *symptoms* that ask for attention and shape one's life in subtle and dramatic ways. Not only do depth psychology's insights "derive from souls in extremis, the sick, suffering, abnormal, and fantastic conditions of psyche," depth psychology owes its origins to the symptomatic psyche.[62] Freud made this plain in one of the essays he wrote in the style of a public lecture, published in 1933 as *The New Introductory Lectures in Psycho-Analysis.* He began by addressing his readers as though they were an assembled audience with these words:

> Ladies and Gentlemen, — I know you are aware in regard to your own relations, whether with people or with things, of the importance of your starting-point. This was also the case with psychoanalysis. It has not been a matter of indifference for the course of its development or for the reception it met with that it began its work on what is, of all the contents of the mind, most foreign to the ego — on symptoms. Symptoms are derived from the repressed, they are, as it were, its representatives before the ego — internal foreign territory — just as reality (if you will forgive the unusual expres-

sion) is external foreign territory. The path led from symptoms, to the unconscious, to the life of the instincts, to sexuality.[63]

The beginning Freud referred to was his work with Josef Breuer and the series of detailed case histories they published in 1895, *Studies on Hysteria*. These first patients confirmed what Freud had begun to suspect; symptoms are meaningful and can be worked through repeatedly in analysis to produce psychological insight. The symptomatic psyche is a fundamental assumption of depth psychology and the symptom is the way psyche attracts attention. It directly led to Freud's theories about the unconscious and modern techniques to explore it. Without the symptom, the notion of psyche would be limited to consciousness, uprooting the soul from the dark and fertile ground of its being. To be true to the psyche, one is obligated to be true to the symptom.

"Whatever else may or may not be said of this unconscious," says Robert Romanyshyn, "it is the self restored to the thickness of flesh and to the depth of the world, a self with a history and a situation."[64] The patients who walk into the therapist's office come with their history, their situation, and above all, their symptoms. These symptoms are useful and meaningful in two ways. They reveal that something is wrong and they also suggest how it could be made right. As such, symptoms are "a way back to what has been forgotten, lost, ignored, or otherwise left behind."[65] Pursue the symptom and find the psyche, suggests James Hillman, because "the symptom is the first herald of an awakening psyche that will not tolerate any more abuse. Through the symptom the psyche demands attention."[66]

The psyche that will tolerate no more abuse, including inattention, reveals itself between the cracks in conscious awareness. The conventional belief was and is that symptoms are random, meaningless disorders that interrupt a rational, orderly life. This is not so at all, said Freud in his essay on the unconscious. It is that all conscious acts that otherwise appear "disconnected and unintelligible . . . fall into a demonstrable connection if we interpolate between them the unconscious acts which we have inferred."[67] In other words, it is the chaotic discontinuity and fragmentary nature of conscious life that points towards an invisible connecting matrix, the unconscious. For the unconscious or partly unconscious individual, which is all people most of the time, the symptom is psyche's herald.

The symptoms that Freud and Jung attended to included physical ail-
ments, psychosomatic illnesses, as well as psychological distress without
physical symptom. For example, one of Freud's cases concerned a woman
who had no feeling in her left hand. He tested the brachial nerves of that
arm, which run from their origin in the cervical spine (the neck) to the
fingertips, and found that they were perfectly healthy. There was no physiological basis, therefore, for the woman's experience of *glove anesthesia* — the
total absence of feeling in the hand but not the arm. Rather than dismiss
this patient's condition, Freud believed that it was real and valid and deserved his medical attention as a doctor of the psyche. The body, he discovered, was a particularly rich medium for psychological expression.

Even today the idea that the psyche is somatic and that the body expresses the psyche is unwelcome in many circles. But at the end of the
nineteenth century, when Victorian repression had reached its peak, it
was deeply subversive. Little wonder. The prevailing attitude, endorsed
by virtually every other medical doctor, continued a two-thousand-year-
old tradition of prizing the intellect and attempting to dominate the body
or ignore it altogether. When Freud and Jung adopted the stance that the
body was a source of vital information with something meaningful to say,
they were true revolutionaries. Partly because this idea was revolutionary
and therefore a dicey subject to address in proper society, Freud made a
strategic decision. In his popular writings, he decided to introduce evidence to prove the existence of the unconscious with a more recognizable
set of symptoms. Thus his collection of introductory lectures on psycho-
analysis begins with lengthy chapters on *parapraxes,* which are slips of the
tongue or pen that would be familiar to a lay audience. Such slips, Freud
carefully argued, are unconscious though purposive mistakes that all individuals make in language and writing. Freud used these lectures to demonstrate two important and related points about his new science. First,
mental health and illness could be visualized as two opposing ends of a
continuum, with so-called normal people existing somewhat toward the
healthy end. Second, all mental (psychic) acts have a purpose and meaning. It's up to the careful observer — that is, a trained analyst like Freud
— to detect that purpose because such a person knows that nothing that
goes on in the psyche is random.

Freud's introductory lectures ultimately ran the gamut of his major theories. In them, he acknowledged that some members of his audience would find his ideas shocking. He was right, of course. In fact, many professionals found Freud's ideas shocking and had done from the very beginning. The source of the controversy was not the attention Freud paid to illness (somatic or psychosomatic), parapraxes, and dreams. It was not even that he popularized such ideas as the unconscious and displaced the ego from its position of hegemony. The source of the controversy was that Freud disturbed the sleep of mankind by demonstrating, using legitimate scientific methodology, just how thin the veneer of civilization truly is. In his essay on the ego and the id, Freud said this:

> If anyone were inclined to put forward the paradoxical proposition that the normal man is not only far more immoral than he believes but also far more moral than he knows, psycho-analysis, on whose findings the first half of the assertion rests, would have no objection to raise against the second half . . . This proposition is only apparently a paradox; it simply states that human nature has a far greater extent, both for good and for evil, than it thinks it has — i.e. than the ego is aware through conscious perception. [68]

The prevailing view that Freud had to combat might be summed up this way: if repressing the symptoms of the psyche helped to maintain the illusion that humanity had truly evolved beyond, or brought under strict control, its base instincts, then so be it. Ignoring a few neurotic individuals was a small price to pay for sustaining the comforting belief in humanity's steady march towards moral and mental superiority. The irony is that Freud, a straight-laced bourgeois who in many respects lived a highly traditional life, refused to obey tradition. He fixed his considerable attention on the neurosis evident in his patients, and the culture at large, and made the symptom the empirical basis of his work.

Like Freud, Jung often described himself as an empiricist who paid attention to the symptoms of the psyche. However, the two men pursued depth psychology in different ways and to different ends in part due to how they defined and treated symptoms. Freud, as we have mentioned earlier, fully embraced the scientific *Weltanschauung* or what we today call classical science. Jung bypassed the distancing stance of classical science in favor of more participatory methods, allying himself with the twentieth century new science of Einstein, Heisenberg, Bohr, and Bohm, among others.

The question of *what* people pay attention to and *how* they attend to it has important implications. Using as an example the glove anesthesia mentioned earlier, Freud tended to focus on bodily symptoms, but his work with hysteria was a profound breakthrough in understanding the body of the psyche. Freud demonstrated that the metaphorical nature of the symptom is even more powerful than anatomical cause-and-effect. That is, the physician's inability to detect a physiological cause for a symptom does not undermine the symptom's legitimacy. Freud thought beyond physiological cause-and-effect to psychological cause-and-effect. If the symptom presents itself, the psychoanalyst is professionally bound to attend to it. Jung focused on archetype, complex, and image, and seems to have been less interested in physical symptoms as manifestations of the psyche. His emphasis on image — manifesting in dreams, fantasies, artwork, and movement — and the importance of image to Jung's analytical psychology has been well established. It is encapsulated in Jung's famously terse definition: *psyche is image*. Paying attention to the image pays attention to the psyche.

Image, for Jung and many Jungians, seems to be ethereal and out-of-body. Hillman suggests this by using spiritual language to describe psyche as a vocation: "The call of soul convinces; it is a seduction into psychological faith, a faith in images and the thought of the heart, into an animation of the world."[69] Some depth psychologists believe that Hillman's emphasis on the imaginal precludes an embodied, emotional response to the psyche, which produces an overintellectualized approach that makes it "impossible to include problems such as unconscious shame, guilt or rage within its purview."[70] We disagree. Living images are highly idiosyncratic and psychoactive, meaning that they stimulate distinct physical and emotional responses, as Hillman explains:

> It is through emotion that we get the exaggerated sense of soul, of honor, of hurt, of anxiety, of our own person. In emotion we get the awareness that we are not alone in ourselves, not in control over all of ourselves, that there is another person, if only an uncon-

scious complex, who also has something — often a great deal — to say about our behavior. So again, the finding of the soul through the unconscious is a stumbling sort of discovery. We fall into emotions, moods, affects, and discover a new dimension which, much as we wish to rid ourselves of, leads us downward into depths of ourselves. [71]

Hillman takes his lead from Jung, in a point Jung made in his late work *Mysterium Coniunctionis*. The soul "tends to favour the body and everything bodily, sensuous, and emotional." [72] Accordingly, the task is to "reconcile ourselves to the mysterious truth that the spirit is the life of the body seen from within, and the body is the outward manifestation of the life of the spirit — the two being really one." It is only then, Jung said, that "we can understand why the striving to transcend the present level of consciousness through the acceptance of the unconscious must give the body its due, and why recognition of the body cannot tolerate a philosophy that denies it in the name of the spirit." [73]

Paying attention to the symptomatic psyche is one of the primary ways people can give the body its due. What do symptoms have to say about the soul? What might the soul be saying by means of the symptom? Jung is correct that a philosophy of denial — soul sacrificed in the name of spirit — is damaging. Hillman makes an equally strong case that a philosophy of treatment — meaning overlooked for the sake of a quick solution — is just as damaging. If people rush to fix the symptom in the wrong-headed attempt to cure the soul of its psychopathology, what might they miss? "Before making moves to treat it, condemn it, justify it, or do anything else for or against it . . . let us stand for the pathological psyche by standing in it long enough to advance our claim that pathologizing is valid, authentic, and necessary." [74]

It is vitally important to accept all of the ways in which psychological insight occurs. The psyche can and does express itself in the physical realm through symptom, sickness, and sensation, in the imaginal realm through image, fantasy, or intuition, and in the mental realm through the idea, the obsession, the delusion, or the thought. Furthermore, since the *anima mundi* or world soul is a key idea in Jungian psychology (absent in Freud), symptoms and sensations, thoughts and intuitions, can and do arise from the things of the world. As we mentioned before, mountains, rivers, trees, and deserts, and also skyscrapers, freeways, prisons, schools and playgrounds are not inert objects without a soul or a voice. They are the more-than-human phenomena of this world that humans must learn to hear.

The degree of receptivity to each and every manifestation of the psyche varies from person to person. The essential point is acknowledging all the ways in which the psyche speaks. Awakening to any of these psychic manifestations may occur gradually or instantaneously. The psyche also has been known to nag, seduce, and importune. The point being, it isn't above getting a person's attention by any workable means.

In any inquiry that values the psyche, attention is essential. One should assume that the psyche is continually producing hints, suggestions, and insights, which flicker at the edge of conscious awareness all the time. It is probably true and it makes for a very rich creative experience. It is all too easy to greet this steady stream of information with a reductive "nothing but" attitude or altogether dismiss it as fantasy. But in treating such information with contempt, one may well be ignoring an inspired source of wisdom.

COMMITMENT 6: THE PSYCHE IS MULTIPLE AND RELATIONAL

Much of the writing in depth psychology refers to basic concepts and theories. It portrays psychic structures such as the id, the ego, the superego, the shadow, anima, animus, and the collective unconscious as constructs that allow the depth psychologist to pay attention to phenomena that would otherwise go unnoticed. A biologist might use a biological construct with a similar goal in mind — to notice, measure, and organize the phenomena he observes, which he then uses to refine his theory. But this scientific approach leaves little room for a relationship between observer and subject except for the most distant, neutral and supposedly objective kind. In science, this is considered the ideal relationship.

In his writing, Freud embraced this ideal relationship and wrote as a medical scientist, maintaining a formal, distant, and conceptual approach to the psyche. This approach is evident in the formal tone and systematic, clear writing style in much of his work. In the Standard Edition of his works, Freud treats the psyche as an object to be inspected and encouraged his patients to be equally distant and objective. Rather than relating *to* the psyche, Freudian psychoanalysis as it is presented via Freud's writing focuses on the relationship *among* the three structures of the psyche, ego, id and superego. Freud portrayed their relationship as a contentious one in which the poor, beleaguered ego deserved both support and sympathy in its ongoing struggle to maintain civility and coherence. In a successful analysis, the patient's ego is ultimately able to dominate the unruly forces that make life so chaotic and demanding. As discussed earlier, some of Freud's most dramatic descriptions of the psyche were couched in the language of strife or battle, which is not surprising. He battled all his life to defend psychoanalysis, which developed in a particular social and political milieu that left its imprint on the infant discipline. This milieu was characterized by paternalism, imperialism, and the deadly competition for land and power that ultimately erupted in two world wars.

Jung's prose is poetic and associative rather than linear and systematic. Unlike Freud, Jung believed that the psyche makes itself known through a variety of means and methods. Revelation and intuition, two of these means, are legitimate sources of knowledge. In many passages of his Collected Works, Jung clearly views the psyche as a living entity rather than as a scientific concept, and advocates a participatory, intimate relationship with psychic phenomena. In addition to the dynamic relationship existing *among* psychic phenomena, the individual can engage in a dynamic relationship *with* the phenomena. The psyche is invisible but quite tangible and an entity one can personally know though never wholly grasp.

To know the contents of the unconscious psyche, such as the shadow, anima, animus and numerous other archetypes as *persons*, the individual must make the first move towards them. Otherwise they will remain merely theoretical constructs, arid images without substance, emotions, preferences, or agendas. Jung's method for approaching the contents of the psyche on a personal basis is called *active imagination*:

> You yourself must enter into the process [of active imagination] with your personal reactions, just as if you are one of the fantasy

figures, or rather, as if the drama being enacted before your eyes were real. It is a psychic fact that this fantasy is happening, and is as real as you — as a psychic entity — are real. If this crucial operation is not carried out, all the changes are left to the flow of images, and you yourself remain unchanged.[75]

Jung was careful to distinguish between two ontological states: a person's reality as a physical being and a person's reality as a psychic being. He was not so naive as to suggest that the imaginal figures who populate the psyche were *physically* real. But they are *psychically* real, and at this level of ontology one can and should engage them. It is the only way to know the multiple figures that comprise the psyche and the only way they will get to know the person.

Jung advocated treating the psyche and the many phenomena it produces as expressive others capable of being addressed and of addressing oneself. To borrow Martin Buber's phrase, one treats the psyche as a "Thou" and not an "it." Psychological life, including psychological inquiry, requires a shift from passive voyeurism to active engagement with these autonomous, idiosyncratic, individual persons. A way to do this is imagining the psyche as Psyche, the young woman from the myth *Eros and Psyche*, and welcoming *her* into the work. When the psyche becomes Psyche, it is a relatively easy step to re-envision psychic contents as psychic persons and begin a relationship with them, a move we discuss in Chapter 4. In psychological inquiry, one relinquishes the habit of observing, categorizing and measuring inert, impersonal objects and instead fosters friendship, familiarity, and even intimacy with the persons who populate the psyche.

Relating to Psyche and psychic images as persons first occurred to Jung at an early age. In his autobiographical work *Memories, Dreams, and Reflections*, he described how understanding anything of a complex nature required participating in an inwardly audible dialogue. From age 12 he began to see himself as consisting of two distinct personalities. Personality 1 was an insecure schoolboy with such traits as

Meanness, vanity, mendacity, and abhorrent egotism . . . Besides *his* world there existed another realm, like a temple in which anyone who entered was transformed and suddenly overpowered by a vision of the whole cosmos so that he could only marvel and admire, forgetful of himself.[76]

This is the realm of the *Other* or Personality 2. Jung stated clearly that he saw this figuring and multiplicity not as an imaginative boy's fanciful notion but as the true nature of psychological experience. "The play and counterplay between personalities 1 and 2, which has run through my whole life, has nothing to do with a 'split' or dissociation in the ordinary medical sense. On the contrary, it is played out in every individual." The relationship between Person 1 and Person 2 is portrayed throughout Jung's writing as a dialectical relationship in which both are needed to make something more. We will have more to say about the dialectical psyche later in this chapter.

Viewing the psyche as a living field populated with persons who engage the individual in dialogue is not as new as one might suspect, nor is it unique to depth psychology. Most creative people are familiar with the experience of the psychic field, though they may not use that language in speaking of it. For thousands of years artists have credited an invisible and ineffable source of their inspiration. Moreover, there has been a distinct tendency to personify this source as feminine. Socrates credited Diotema[77] and poets and writers throughout the ages have often referred to *her* as The Muse. Thus, individuals engaged in psychological inquiry easily may find themselves thinking of Psyche as a person and a partner in the work. To do so continues a long and venerable tradition that honors the organic sense that creators and their work exist within a living matrix of inspiration and wisdom encompassing what one can see and measure as well as what one can feel and intuit.

It should be evident that those who welcome the psyche already are obeying the third philosophical commitment of depth psychology — that the psyche is personal and more-than-personal. Humanity exists within it. Jung used the Latin term *unus mundus* to describe the infinite, invisible, and living psychic field that envelops and constitutes the world. It also is referred to as the *anima mundi*, which makes explicit that the world itself has a soul and all phenomena within it are ensouled. Welcoming the psyche obligates people to accept the reality of the psyche as an infinite living field and to view their creative work as an exploration of one part of the field. Through such exploration, they gradually come to know the psyche as a living being. Or, to put it in poetic terms, the psyche will respond to this dedicated attention in the way a flower opens to the sun, by revealing more of its beauty and fullness.

Jung discovered that it was the alchemists' sustained association with the invisible forces of the psyche that was the real secret of their work.[78] The invitation to the psyche is not extended once and that's all. Rather, the invitation is a continual posture of welcome over weeks and months, which can become a lifelong practice. This welcoming posture is what Jung often referred to as a "good attitude." A former patient of Jung's described it this way:

> By keeping quiet, repressing nothing, remaining attentive, and by accepting reality — taking things as they are, and not as I wanted them to be — by doing all this, unusual knowledge has come to me, and unusual powers as well, such as I could never have imagined before . . . So now I intend to play the game of life, being receptive to whatever comes to me, good and bad, sun and shadow forever alternating, and, in this way, also accepting my own nature with its positive and negative sides. Thus everything becomes more alive to me.[79]

There are two principles embedded in this statement. The first principle is to be *attentive* to whatever phenomenon appears exactly as it appears. The second principle is to *accept* whatever phenomenon appears exactly as it appears. What emerges from the psyche requires "a certain tender care . . . as well as waiting, pausing, listening [that] takes a span of time and a tension of patience . . . *This attitude is what the soul needs in order to be felt and heard.*"[80]

Depth psychologists describe their relationship to the psyche as one in which hospitality is paramount. The classical Jungian attitude toward the dream, for instance, calls for welcoming figures and images that present themselves much as a gracious host welcomes her guests. Mary Watkins, who wrote a seminal work describing this attitude, titled her book *Invisible Guests*.

> If we begin, as Jung did, with a respect for the imaginal other . . .
> then the activities of the imagining ego need not be de-personifica-
> tion, de-potentiation, reclamation and assimilation — but instead
> the building of relationships in dialogue. The self does not attempt
> to abolish the autonomous presence of the other . . . Development
> occurs in the dialogue between self and other. [81]

The extended metaphor of hospitality offers many insights into a person's relationship to the psyche. There is, as mentioned earlier, an emphasis on gracious welcome. Skilled hosts are generous, open-minded,
and magnanimous; not tight, mean-spirited, or pusillanimous. They also
will do their best to draw out all of the guests, helping them feel at ease
and comfortable expressing themselves. Such a host will be inquisitive
without being overbearing, wanting to enjoy each guest as a distinct and
interesting character. Under the encouraging warmth of this style of welcome, images produced by the psyche will fully present themselves.

Watkins emphasizes the dialogical nature of the relationship between
ego and imaginal guest. An image for this might be a nineteenth-century
literary salon, in which a lively exchange of views and ideas enriches, inspires, and entertains the guests. Such an image vivifies a point we discussed earlier in this chapter, people are not single-minded. They naturally are comprised of many emotions, beliefs, values, feelings, moods,
and modes of being, which they can imagine as the visitation of various
archetypes or gods: Aries when they are angry, Demeter when they are
maternal, and Hermes when they are quick-witted. The task of the psychological individual is to welcome this diversity without prejudice or
repression, much in the same way that a skilled host creates a comfortable setting for guests. From the perspective of archetypal psychology, the
multiple persons of the psyche do not indicate pathology. It is the way the
dynamic psyche expresses its natural multiplicity. "Each imaginal figure
provides a different perspective through which events and the self itself
can be viewed" [82] which adds valuable flexibility to the art of inquiry.

The idea of hosting the multiple persons of the psyche originates in
Jung's early experiences with the fantasy figures who showed up in his
dreams, visions, and artwork. During his frightening confrontation with

the unconscious after he and Freud parted ways, Jung was slowly introduced to the reality of the psyche and the autonomy of psychic persons.

> Philemon and other figures of my fantasies brought home to me
> the crucial insight that there are things in the psyche which I do
> not produce, but which produce themselves and have their own
> life. Philemon represented a force which was not myself. In my
> fantasies I held conversations with him, and he said things which I
> had not consciously thought. For I observed clearly that it was he
> who spoke, not I . . . It was he who taught me psychic objectivity,
> the reality of the psyche. [83]

As more fantasy figures began to visit Jung, he felt frightened and overwhelmed. Fifteen years later, a conversation with an Indian scholar about
his own guru who regularly appeared to this man despite the fact that
he had been dead for centuries, reassured Jung. He began to understand
the presence of Philemon and other fantasy figures in his life as "the sort
of thing that could happen to others who made similar efforts." [84] Over
the course of his life he continued taking such persons seriously and welcomed their perspectives and insights.

Adopting a welcoming attitude toward psychic persons provides an
experience of the multiple psyche and compelling evidence of the psyche's
autonomy. Furthermore, it encourages one to relate to the psyche as
Psyche — just as one would regard any other good friend. It also asks the
person to expect the same kind of willfulness, individuality, sensitivity,
reactivity, creativity, and self-expression from the psyche as one expects
from another human being.

Regarding the psyche as Psyche, a person, has profound repercussions. First, it means that Psyche is a partner in any endeavor, "the very
source of the creative impulse." It is the more-than-personal "deposit of
all human experience right back to its remotest beginnings . . . a living
system of reactions and aptitudes that determine the individual's life in
invisible ways — all the more effective because invisible." [85] If one ignores
or forgets that creative work is truly a partnership with the living Psyche,
whatever one produces will be unpsychological. It may be laudable for
other reasons, but it won't honor Psyche.

COMMITMENT 7: THE PSYCHE IS COMPLEX AND CONTRADICTORY

The postmodern era has been called an *age of disbelief.* It is a time characterized by a deeply situated skepticism and by a consequent loss of belief
in any possibility of objective reality, first principles, or absolute truth.
It is a time of complexity and contradiction — a time of deconstructed
systems of thought. In all fairness to the history of ideas we should acknowledge that the postmodern critique is not new to the philosophical scene. One can find rich criticisms of objective reality as far back as
Plato's dialogues in the figure of Protagoras and the Sophists attempting
to discredit Socrates ideas about truth. In one way or another there has
been a healthy debate about what may constitute truth or reality as long
as claims to knowledge have been made. Perhaps the postmodern versions of this critical approach seem more radical, both because they are
current and because they assault claims to truths that have been made
more forcefully and prolifically than any, ever before.

The terms of the postmodern argument are new and more richly im-
bued with technical proof and contradiction. That fact of the argument is,
we believe, given with the psyche. It is the nature of the psyche to be complex and contradictory beyond any ultimate settlement of what is true.
Further, the more one examines the reasonable resting places of postmodern thought the more they resemble an acknowledgment that all claims to
knowing must allow for complexity and prepare for contradiction.

Depth psychologists have made the peculiar move of founding their
field of study on this shifting psychic ground and have consequently provided a way to see the current landscape of intellectual chaos as a kind
of psychological homecoming. Central to both Freud and Jung's idea of
the psyche is the notion that people are only aware of a tiny fraction of
what shapes their values, beliefs, and behavior. This conscious fragment
is embedded within an unconscious whole. The psyche, which is variously
equated with the mind (primarily in Freud) and the soul (primarily in
Jung), includes a spectrum of states of awareness that extends from the
conscious to the unconscious. By paying attention to the entire spectrum
of consciousness, Freud and Jung discovered evidence that the psyche is
naturally composed of multiple parts that interact with one another in a

complex manner — even in healthy people who possess stable, coherent personalities. Since Freud and Jung, many Freudian and Jungian authors have discussed the complex nature of the psyche, frequently speaking of it in archetypal terms. For example, Christine Downing, who has written several books on myth and archetypes, says:

> I have learned that recognition of the archetypal and universal dimensions of one's experiences can help free one from a purely personal relation to them. I also believe that one can celebrate the mythic patternings without losing an appreciation of the concrete and unique moments that constitute one's existence. This is what Freud meant by transference — knowing that one is Sigmund Freud and Oedipus, that I am Christine Downing and Persephone. Either description alone is insufficient.[86]

The meaning of life is enriched by understanding its archetypal roots, its basis in myth. Without sacrificing any sense of uniqueness one can connect with universal patterns of human experience that dramatize the true complexity of the individual psyche.

Though Freud and Jung agreed on the complexity of the psyche, each man mapped its landscape differently and devised distinct terminology to define its principle features. Freud favored a more structured, hierarchical approach to the psyche than Jung. The early Freud drew the psyche as an oval, with a preconscious, a conscious (ego) and a personal unconscious, which he later came to equate with the id. The later Freud used a similar ovoid shape and spoke of the id, ego and superego, each having their own agenda. (As scholars have noted, one way to trace the evolution in Freud's thinking is by observing the transformation of the maps he used to refer to psychical structures.) Freud described the relationship among the parts of the psyche as dynamic, which he frequently depicted as inherently competitive. It is the ego's task to mediate among the competing demands of the complex psyche. "An action by the ego is as it should be if it satisfies simultaneously the demands of the id, of the super-ego and of reality — that is to say, if it is able to reconcile their demands with one another."[87] However, Freud was not confident in the ego's ability to do so. Individuals often have the experience of being internally divided because they are subject to the centrifugal force of the different parts of the psyche. These parts of the psyche are not entirely distinct. They tend to blend into one another, acting as interrelated, dynamic processes more than separate, rigid structures. Thus one aspect of Freudian psychodynamic theory — the idea that the psyche consists of different structures each with its own agenda — rests upon the assumption of the psyche's complexity.

There is another way in which Freudian psychoanalysis rests on the assumption of a complex and contradictory psyche. Complexity exists *within* the psyche's structures. Whereas the ego tends towards coherence and logical order, Freud alludes to the fact that the conscious mind only approaches unity or uniformity. "Perhaps there is room in the mind for contrary purposes, for contradictions, to exist side by side."[88] The superego also is complex and contradictory since it is the distillation of many voices of authority that may or may not agree with one another. It is first formed in response to the parents, but "in the course of an individual's development, receives contributions from later successors and substitutes of his parents, such as teachers and models in public life of admired social ideals."[89] The id is an altogether different phenomenon from either the ego or the superego. It is "a chaos, a cauldron full of seething excitations" that has "no organization [and] produces no collective will." In the id, "contrary impulses exist side by side, without canceling each other out or diminishing each other."[90]

Jung never mapped the psyche *per se*, but he frequently spoke of the psyche's wholeness and used the circle to symbolize this. He did not use this symbol, however, to imply that the psyche was a unified phenomenon. As Jung puts it, "the psyche is not a unity, but a contradictory multiplicity of complexes."[91] Fissures in the psyche, which are openings through which unconscious content may present itself, reveal the psyche's fragmentary nature. These fissures intrigue depth psychologists because they are the starting point for inquiry into soul.

Jung's belief in the complexity of the psyche began with his early research using the word association test. When he spoke a stimulus word to a patient, he observed that the person responding was "not master in his own house" but instead under the influence of something *other* with a distinct personality of its own. Jung noted that the patient's reactions would be delayed, altered, suppressed, or replaced by these "autonomous intruders." From this he developed the theory of the *complex*, a concept he introduced into depth psychology:

> Whenever a stimulus-word touches something connected with the hidden complex, the reaction of the conscious ego will be disturbed, or even replaced, by an answer coming from the complex. It is just as if the complex were an autonomous being capable of interfering with the intentions of the ego. Complexes do indeed behave like secondary or partial personalities possessing a mental life of their own. [92]

Jung equated his notion of the complex to the earlier theory of the fixed subconscious idea introduced by Pierre Janet. Janet, along with his teacher Charcot, had done pioneering work with multiple personalities in the nineteenth century. Jung's contribution was to discover that even the normal human psyche is complex and contradictory. In both the mentally healthy and the mentally ill, sub-personalities emerge that tend to be distinct, autonomous and willful. He called these autonomous sub-personalities "complexes," and found that they are not inherently pathological. Everybody has them. In fact, complexes "contain the driving power of psychic life [without which] psychic activity would come to a fatal standstill." [93]

The complex became the basic structural element in Jung's map of the psyche, a clear testament to its complexity. Even the ego, which Jung defined as the center of the field of consciousness, is a complex. As the more-or-less conscious component of the psyche that gives the individual an enduring and stable sense of self, the ego is obliged to acknowledge, and relate to, the multiple persons that naturally inhabit complex psychic life. Frequently, what is most repulsive to an order-seeking ego is chaos. People are admired and rewarded for being decisive, which all too often means quickly eliminating alternatives and repressing complexity. It is just this tendency that the multiple psyche seeks to compensate.

The psychological individual can learn to welcome rather than shun everything unknown, no matter how repulsive, messy, or complicated it may be. Receptivity to the psyche in all its manifestations requires a paradoxical attitude capable of holding the tension of the opposites. As Marie-Louise von Franz explains, a paradoxical attitude makes it possible to be receptive to the psyche, and receptivity to the psyche accustoms the individual to paradox.

> Clearly there are two possibilities of consciousness, namely a rigid one and one which has a paradoxical attitude and therefore does justice to the paradoxical factor of the unconscious. The latter would be what you could call a consciously open system, an open Weltanschauung which is always ready to accept its opposite, or meet the opposite and accept its contradictions. If you have a conscious attitude which is ready to accept the opposite, to accept the conflict and the contradiction, then you can connect with the unconscious. [94]

What von Franz calls "connecting with the unconscious" is what we have described as welcoming the psyche. It is, as she says, a readiness to accept the inevitable conflicts and contradictions of real life.

One might ask why conflict and contradiction are inevitable. The answer, according to Jungian theory, is that the unconscious compensates for the conscious attitude. Often this amounts to contradicting one's most cherished beliefs and attitudes and exposing the complexities in human behavior that one prefers to forget, repress, or simply not know. By showing the other side of things, the unconscious foments potential conflicts. This is one of the ways the psyche demands attention. Another result of conflict and contradiction is the widening of consciousness, which is the aim of psychological life and the means by which it occurs. Contradiction opens up a gap between opposing ideas and at the same time firmly establishes the relationship between them. Seeing the relationship, or seeking a way across the gap (which is not necessarily the same thing), stimulates further inquiry. We discuss the gap and its implications for psychological inquiry in the eighth philosophical commitment, next.

The idea of a complex and contradictory psyche is closely linked to another of Jung's key ideas, the principle of *enantiodromia*. According to this principle, any idea, thesis, attitude, or activity pursued to its endpoint will lead to its antithesis. Enantiodromia is part of the psyche's balancing act, a kind of self-correcting mechanism that illustrates the cyclical and circular nature of wholeness. We noticed it, for example, as we were writing this book. Once we made a clear, decisive statement about the psyche or on behalf of the psyche, other voices and other ideas appeared at the periphery of our attention wanting their turn. It's something like actors waiting in the wings for their entrance onto the lighted stage. Though this energetic interplay of ideas can seem annoying or distracting, it fuels the creative process. The dynamic fluctuation is natural to the psyche and it is this pattern of movement, more than any other attribute, which demonstrates the psyche's holistic aim.

We have found that it is helpful to think of the complexity of the psyche in archetypal terms. Every archetype, or god, has its own distinct character, and with that character comes a set of values, behaviors and ideas. Focus, for instance, can be thought of as an Apollonian trait. When one's perspective is captivated by Apollo, psychological inquiry will be pure, efficient, objective, and intentional; that is, there is an aim to pursue, and pursue one must. Many people find themselves quite Apollonian in articulation of a particular point, like right now, in our attempt to *clarify* Apollo. (Apollo loves to be clear.) But as we write we're aware that dancing at the edge of awareness is a whole host of other ideas that, if we were to indulge them right now, would mess up the clarity of the explanation. That's Hermes, Apollo's brother. Hermes is the adventurous and undisciplined sibling who gets into everything, making lightning-quick connections between one idea and another. In some cases, of course, Hermes leads people down a false trail just for the sheer joy of the journey. But is it false? Here is where the ability to be flexible — to switch allegiance and follow another god —can be surprisingly fruitful. The clarity of Apollo conjures the playful wanderlust of Hermes. The task is to recognize this as a legitimate and worthwhile part of creative work. Every archetype is a fragment of the whole. Propitiating the gods who visit and the gods one wants to have visit is a way of seeking that wholeness.

COMMITMENT 8: THE PSYCHE IS DIALECTICAL

Reflection on all of the previous philosophical commitments of depth psychology reveals an interesting pattern of ideas. Once one declares that Psyche is real — the primary datum and ontological beginning place — one finds that subsequent commitments have a consistent leaning toward complexity, creativity, and motion. Then when one views the psyche as characterologically, spatially, or developmentally differentiated, as occurs whenever one posits an unconscious in relation to consciousness or an ego in relation to a Self, there arises a need for motion and engagement. In the Freudian tradition, as discussed in the context of the protean psyche, the theories of psychodynamics carry this idea of motion. Jung and his followers use a variety of metaphors, including alchemy, the interplay of archetypal forces, imagination, and individuation. What becomes clear is that inquiry that hopes to be psychological must take into account this characteristic of movement. Methods must simply learn to move, even dance, if they are to follow psyche. In the remainder of this chapter we examine some of those dance steps. Above all, we notice that the psyche favors a particular rhythm, the rhythm of dialectics.

The word dialectics derives from the Greek *dialektike*, which was a particular kind of speaking aimed at explanatory discourse. As a word, dialectic has been a bit of a troublemaker. It has moved into and out of favor in philosophical discourse and has shifted and added meanings without much regard for the confusion that might engender. It is all the more alluring because of this fluidity; it becomes a word that actually seems to dance to its own tune. In this book, we too are inclined to dance, and so we will give the word our own spin. It is a spin that has roots in Plato, branches out in the work of Georg W. F. Hegel (1770–1831), and leafs out more fully in the work of Hans Georg Gadamer.

Dialectic is not explanation. Rather, it is a circumambulating exchange of ideas that arrives at its truth prudently and intentionally, but indirectly. In the classical Greek tradition, dialectics as a pedagogical technique is commonly attributed to the master, Socrates, as rendered in the *Dialogues of Plato*. Later definitions have tended to limit the meaning of dialectic to the idea of progressive argumentation or refutation as a matter of actual speech between two people. However it is important for our story to retain Plato's sense, particularly referenced in the *Sophist*, that this kind of speech is inseparable from thought itself in that both are naturally conversational.

In Plato, and later in Hegel, dialectics serves to illuminate a potentially deeper or superior meaning — like a third thing. It is a kind of spiritual practice that leads to a truth that is pleasing to the gods. In Platonic philosophy this resolving movement of dialectics was a necessary response to the problem of a separation between the real and the ideal — the immortal form and mortal capacity to live it out. Perhaps the most repeated theme in the dialogues of Plato is that there is a permanent divide between earthly beings and the divine and that only the philosopher can hope to bridge it.[95] This divide or gap is the paradoxical capacity to imagine and hold deep faith with that which one seems to know, even though it cannot be proved or measured in the realm called reality.

In a larger sense, the gap is nothing less than the source of psychological life. The existence of the word *reality* and its root word *real* conjures its *others*, including the words ideal, unreal, imaginary or imaginal, and fictional. The gap between real and unreal that Plato articulates is the mother of all gaps including the gap between good and evil, upper world and under world, truth and confusion, transcendent and mundane, conscious and unconscious and so on. It is a gap that is so embedded in the philosophy and psychology of the Western mind that one could even say that depth psychology is a *psychology of the gap*.

It is this gap or differentiation within the thought frame that gives rise to so much that we say here about the lived experience of Psyche. But the gap also calls for a way across it. This way is the way of dialectics.

In modern times Hegel carried on a rigorous and hopeful project to articulate the practice of dialectics and present it as a natural philosophy of the psyche. Like Kant, Hegel acknowledged the role of the mind in the construction of reality. Hegel saw the ongoing dialectical activity of confronting perception, idea, critique, and understanding as the nature of truth, not an imperfect human attempt to gain truth. He articulated a view of the psyche and the world as implicitly dialectical. In this view all human thought and nature itself is composed of paradox and contradic-

tion but not in the pejorative sense of those terms. Rather, Hegel defend-
ed paradox and contradiction as the source of the natural and necessary
movement that arises from any mixing of thoughts, images, and ideas. In
that mix, paradox and contradiction are the stirring spoons of psyche, of
being in the world.

Hegel's work on dialectics was an immense philosophical shift in
Western thought. It promised to unite the practice of reason with the
realm of the irrational, not as the enemies, but as objects of desire. Hegel's
dialectic acknowledged the gap without leaving people in the angst of
separation. Instead, he invited them to experience doubt, confusion, and
contradiction as the necessary ingredients of an unfolding dialectical synthesis. For Hegel, truth and the methods of attaining it could retain some
measure of paradox because the mind is capable of comprehending it.

In the postmodern era Hegel's work has been criticized and widely
discredited primarily for its roots in the romantic philosophical tradition
and for its teleological commitment. Hegel was explicitly committed to
an evolutionary view of humanity. The necessity that drives Hegelian dialectic is ultimately a theological argument and it carries a Western, even
Christian revelation of God's plan for mankind. But though it would
likely be displeasing to Hegel, his view of the dialectical world does not
require the postulation of an evolutionary goal or divine plan. Hegel's
description of the movements of the dialectical psyche can stand alone
simply as the way of things and how one knows them.

Following Hegel, others picked up various threads of the dialectical
project. Marx and Engels, for example, developed their theory of *dialectical
materialism* while in another part of the world the American psychologist
William James advocated the nineteenth-century philosophy of pragma-
tism. These efforts often fell into the same trap that caught Hegel. They
aligned themselves with an end vision or telos so that the dialectic was
aimed toward some sort of developmental or evolutionary end and not
simply a natural, rhythmic movement between ideas, values, and images.
One current resurgence of Hegelian thought has emerged right within
the community of Jungian scholars and depth psychological theorists.
Through its critique it has given new vitality to the realm of archetypal
psychology. Wolfgang Giegerich, both a philosopher and a Jungian ana-

lyst, has taken depth psychology, and particularly his own field of Jungian psychology, to task for being intellectually lazy for its failure to continue what he sees as psychology's primary task, an exploration of the logical life of the soul. In his book, *The Soul's Logical Life* he sets himself a corrective task, "I want to push archetypal psychology with its imaginal approach forward beyond the half-way mark at which it stopped."[96] Giegerich takes the position that the soul's being is rooted not in its contents or images but in the bridging action of dialectical thought. Most important in his criticism is that this thought, or logical life, has a forward movement toward greater truth. In other words, he suggests that the dialectical or logical life of the soul is progressive and he criticizes psychology for being regressive with its backward gaze on myth, culture, and history. Inevitably, Giegerich's view of the dialectical psyche recalls the Hegelian passion for a goal or *telos*.

We suggest that the value of a telos lies more in its mythic sense than in some literal line of development. By myth we mean an evocative fiction that, by virtue of its being psychologically true, draws one to its conclusion. The desire for a telos or final destination of the psyche is a psychological necessity that one needn't translate into literal necessity. In fact, the more the telos is literalized, the less psychologically valuable it is. As a myth, however, it is enormously valuable. It always alludes to place not yet visited, an idea not yet comprehended, a world not yet perfected, a form of enlightenment not yet attained. As myth, telos encapsulates the desire and longing that fuels the movement of the dialectical psyche. As myth, telos keeps the dialectical psyche ready for what is needed now, and every moment of "now" that succeeds this one. As myth, telos discourages one from literalizing a natural or divine goal for psyche, a stopping place. It helps one to resist becoming located and fixed in a temporal or culturally-bound political idea. The myth of telos keeps the psyche in movement; or, more to the point, keeps people moving in accord with the natural flux of psyche. In the end the telos, or goal, of a dialectical psyche is to continue its dialectical movement.

In the 1960s the German philosopher, Hans Georg Gadamer revisited the work of Hegel on dialectics. In *Truth and Method: Elements of a Philosophical Hermeneutics*, Gadamer advocated dialectics as an ontology, a way of *being in the world* in the Heideggerian sense. Dialectics, he said, "designates the basic movement of human existence, made up of its finitude and historicality." Therefore dialectics "encompasses the whole of [the individual's] experience of the world." It is evident that Gadamer's dialectic is less a technique and more a consequence of existence in a world full of gaps that create the desire for bridges. The movement of understanding, he says, "is encompassing and universal."[97] Moreover, understanding is a participatory activity where the participation is as natural as, say, breathing. As such, any method or way of understanding should flow from one's very being. If method does not follow character, then it will have no hope of revealing character. One's character, one's being in the world, and the psyche itself, are all essentially dialectical.

Gadamer's work with hermeneutics portrays understanding at the level of day-to-day experience and not at the conceptual level. In this, he followed others in the tradition of phenomenology. Still, much of what is written about dialectics focuses on processes of thinking and can appear, at times, too abstract. The psyche manifests itself in many ways other than thought, including in the life of the body. Trusting in this, we offer a way of seeing the central image of the dialectical psyche in a very few moments of embodied thought. We invite you to do something you can't *not* do, but we ask you to do so with unnatural attention. We invite the act of breathing.

> Sit or stand in a comfortable way and simply take in a breath slowly and consciously. Do not hold the breath or breathe excessively deeply but only slowly enough to allow for this focused attention. Exhale in the same way. Set up a slow rhythmic cycle of breathing that allows for attention. As you do this try to locate the body's great desire to breathe. Notice that at the end of each inhaled breath the desire shifts from wanting to inhale to wanting to exhale. Notice the point of this shift and imagine it to be the end point of the arc of a pendulum, a steady swing back and forth. Each swing is uniquely itself. Notice how differently it feels to breathe in as opposed to how if feels to breathe out. Yet also notice how the end of the inhaled breath gives itself up so willingly to the beginning of the exhaled breath.

The powerful desire to inhale is quietly forgotten as you remember the powerful desire to exhale and vice versa. In such a way it is possible to spend large amounts of time unaware of the entire business of breathing — to become unconscious of your body's great desire to breathe in and to breathe out. You simply forget that in satisfying the desire for one thing you give birth to the desire for the other. It is possible, of course, to conceive of breathing as single cyclical act, which it is. Breathing in and breathing out are so mutually dependent that it makes sense to see them as one thing. But if you truly remember each desire — the way that the desire to inhale has its own particular quality, which, though forceful, is different from the desire to exhale — then it is evident that the body teaches people how to host the dialectical psyche and its world full of *ones* made of *twos*.

The body is full of such dialectical processes. People are born with two eyes that provide a visual argument in favor of depth perspective. Likewise two ears, and two hands; people have two feet and two arms to swing as they walk with them. The very skin reminds people of their cellular level concern with distinguishing between the inner and the outer worlds. But at the same time, the skin, like that neutral moment of arc in the pendulum of breathing, is a reminder that the boundary is necessarily permeable and not so easy to define.

The body provides an ongoing reminder of the feel of the deeper rhythms of the psyche. Of course this modest object lesson is not new, most people have had some exposure to it along the way. But perhaps it is a valuable reminder here, where it underscores the point that the idea of dialectical rhythms is more than just a pertinent metaphor for psychic life — it is the literal way of things from the perspective of psyche. Note we refer to the plural *rhythms* here because we are not dealing with a single or primary dialectic when we talk of a dialectical psyche. Rather, the best image would be that of a fantastic clockwork of dialectical pendulums swinging in an infinite number of arcs and periods, all influencing each other, forever and timeless. In a sense each person lives every moment in an embodied movement of enantiodromia.

The entity of the pair is pervasive in the body and the imagination. However, there is nothing in this view that seeks to privilege pairs over larger groups. We simply want to acknowledge a kind of back and forth movement and the tendency for something clearly articulated to long for its inarticulate other. A second criticism, noted by Gadamer, is that the "I-Thou" image of the dialectical psyche is sometimes unduly circumscribed within a personalistic or person-centered frame. This tendency must be overcome in a depth psychology. Recall that each personal mind is in the psyche and not the other way round. People tend to hold conversations in thought and image because that is psyche's, and also the world's, way of knowing and being.

Let us move from the personal then, and take the ebb and flow of ideas themselves through this dialectical perspective. Ideas are not the property of the thinker but rather hold each thinker in their sway. If that is so then perhaps ideas posses their own real being, have "I-Thou" relationships to each other, and like air they are breathed in and out. Then one might begin to see how some very compelling ideas can, as noted earlier, emerge on the scene, take a prominent position, and then begin to constellate their seeming opposites in a kind of rhythmic dialogue. Such a dialogue or discourse holds humanity's attention for a time, inspires new ways of thinking, and reverberates with old thought. Then perhaps the whole business goes back into background and becomes a kind of obvious given, like breathing, not needing particular attention. In this way ideas are never wholly new but rather are remembrances and recombinations of themselves, just as all fleshy creatures are. So much of Jung's view of the psyche was based on this dynamic of recycling — ideas birthing ideas, consciousness arising from unconsciousness and vice versa — which he experienced over and over again. In a reflection on his sense of re-discovering the world's existence while walking in the East African bush he wrote, "Nothing can exist without its opposite; the two were one in the beginning and will be one again in the end. Consciousness can only exist through continual recognition of the unconscious, just as everything that lives must pass through many deaths."[98]

In closing we return to the image of the dialectical psyche as an infinitely complex clockwork fascinated by its own riddles and tickled by its capacity for discovery, forgetting, and remembrance. But in this clockwork let us focus on the energy and swing of the pendulums more than on the gears. It is not so much a clock keeping time in a chronological or developmental sense but rather in a polyrhythmic and cyclic sense in which the ebb and flow of one set of ideas and attitudes crosses paths with other sets of ideas and attitudes at various times and places. The immense complexity of this image is extended both inward and outward as its movements are taking place not only at the personal level but in the community, the culture, the more than human world and throughout the cosmos. In psychological inquiry the special task is not merely to answer questions at their surfaces but to see how these deeper rhythms of thought and feeling interweave to shape not only answers but also the very natures of the questions themselves. For this one must learn to dance with the dialectical psyche.

The depth psychological perspective discussed in these eight philosophical commitments provides a meaningful and dynamic approach to inquiry. This perspective, in fact depth psychology itself, is at home in the borderland between the known and the yet-to-be-known (which also includes things that never will be fully known). Here one becomes aware of the creative tension between consciousness and the unconscious, exterior surface and interior depth, and the literal and symbolic which stimulates the human imagination and the quest for knowledge, insight and wisdom.

The depth psychological perspective recalls the partial nature of knowledge and consciousness, encouraging the person engaged in inquiry to remain humble in the face of all that can be known. As L. L. Whyte pointed out, there is real danger in total obsession with partial ideas. Psychological inquiry, which pays as much attention to the unique and particular as to the conventional and general, helps individuals avoid this obsession. In psychological inquiry one remains alert to the other thing, to what one doesn't see now, or hasn't sensed yet.

Adopting a depth psychological perspective on inquiry means adopting the ways of the psyche. The psyche is naturally fluid and dynamic and one's attitude should reflect this. Be inclusive, discriminating, precise, penetrating, intimate, distant, hot, cool, insatiable, selective, malleable, reserved, categorical, or impressionable, flexibly adopting any or all of these postures to produce a richer yield of information and understanding. The psyche also is relational. Seek to know and to be known, and relinquish the illusion of sterile objectivity. Psychological inquiry is a

commitment of the whole person and, as a result, the work will be unpre-
dictable, confusing, difficult, satisfying and possibly transformational.

The next two chapters discuss the extensive nature of psychological inquiry and its demands upon and ramifications for the researcher.
Chapter 4 describes moves to invite the psyche into the work as a guide
and partner, whereas Chapter 5 outlines the stages of research and suggests answers to some common questions asked by people engaged in
the art of inquiry.

4

THE MOVES OF PSYCHOLOGICAL INQUIRY

Practice means the things one does — the steps, the processes, and the moves. In most approaches to inquiry there is a tendency to formalize and articulate the practice so that it becomes an identifiable method. Etymologically the word *method* refers to the way over, across, or through. It is a pathway marked by previous travelers and known to be reliable. In conducting an inquiry, the method is often seen as being of equal importance to the results. A trustworthy method vouches for the results and it also reveals the life of the study, the actual modes of encounter, and to some extent the very character of the person using it. Perhaps even more importantly, critical appraisal can reveal how a method shapes what one thinks of as real and not real. Change the method and reality itself can shift. This critical approach to method is often called *methodology*, or the logos of method. It is a way of understanding the method from a philosophical and epistemological standpoint. To engage in methodology is not only to articulate one's method at the level of process, but also to see it limned against the background of similar, related, and different methods — to locate the work in a tradition of scholarly inquiry that expresses how one comes to know what one knows.

Psychologists have a long history of using borrowed methods when conducting scholarly inquiry. Some have felt more affinity for scientific approaches, experimental designs, and quantifiable data that tend to produce broad or general theories, abstracted from the context of lived experience. They are indebted to the natural sciences for their methods. Other psychologists view psychology as a social science because it focuses on human beings. They might be more inclined toward qualitative research, which emphasizes context. Both realms, social science and natural science, yield valuable understandings about human nature. But alignment with the methods of either one, without a critical and psychologically astute methodology, leads to costly and unnecessary reductions of complex lived experiences — the very things that make a depth psychological perspective unique and valuable.

Within method there is another level of practice, which is the level of *moves*. Moves are the actual operations — the turns, starts, and stops, the gathering and arrangement of ideas, words, and concepts — that one makes. Rather than write another book on method in the human sciences, of which there are many and many of them quite good, we have chosen to focus on the moves one might make to keep inquiry richly psychological. We base these moves, to a large extent, on the philosophical commitments of depth psychology. They come about from asking the question, "How might one approach the familiar practices of inquiry, but from the added perspective of depth psychology, so that the moves are *psyche friendly*?"

As we describe the moves in this chapter it will be important to see them not as formulaic or necessarily sequential. Research projects naturally progress through a series of clear stages, the subject of Chapter 5, from developing a preliminary idea through finalizing the manuscript, regardless of what specific method or approach one uses to explore their topic. The moves, however, can occur in any sequence or combination in all projects that begin with a genuine question and are continuously permeated by the spirit of inquiry. They include welcoming the psyche, engaging in ritual, maintaining separation, working through transference, hosting dialogue, collaboration and isolation, presentation and representation, and reflections on language. This collection is only a beginning, which we trust will inspire readers to conceive of other similar moves useful for psychological inquiry. The list is potentially endless.

WELCOMING THE PSYCHE

The foundation for psychological inquiry rests on one essential move, without which all other moves have no sense or meaning: welcoming the psyche. Though it may seem rather obvious, this move is an extensive and subtle undertaking comprised of quite specific attitudes, gestures, and intentions. It asks people to be fully psychological in the traditional sense of that word: to put the psyche at the center of their work. From the moment the inquiry begins until the day it ends, nothing is dismissed as meaning-less, random, or inconsequential. On the contrary, "all things, every object and every action, take on significance to soul."[99] It is essential to inquire of any event, person, dream, emotion, image, mood, thought, insight, or fascination, "What might this have to do with my work?" The answer may be "nothing." But the question needs to be asked nonetheless.

Welcoming psyche to the work is based on the first philosophical commitment of depth psychology: the psyche is real. This move acknowl-edges the existence of the psyche at the personal level, as in "I have a psyche," and also at the objective (collective) level, as in "the psyche exists everywhere" or "the psyche is more than personal," or even "I exist within the psyche." The second part of this commitment — the notion that the psyche exists independently of the human mind — dramatically affects all creative encounters. By granting ontological status to the psyche people forfeit the idea that they are working in a vacuum or inventing ideas out of thin air. Like water to a fish or air to mammals, the psyche is the me-dium that all persons, not just the creative person, inhabits so intimately that one often doesn't even recall its existence. It is no coincidence that the Greek word for soul, psyche, originally meant breath.

Though welcoming the psyche into the work may seem easy, it is not. It is especially difficult for the person who has carved out a bit of in-tellectual territory, chosen a direction in which to move forward, or for whatever reason, is feeling tense, impatient, and dictatorial. Anyone who invites Psyche into the work consciously relinquishes absolute control, just as taking on a human partner is a decision to share authority. Of course, the idea of absolute control in creative work is illusory. Nonethe-less, it is painful to sacrifice this illusion because the desire for control is so very seductive, especially when the work displays its autonomy as a psychic being. As a creative partner, the autonomous psyche is exciting and inspiring, demanding and irritating. But the psyche is not an easy partner for an orderly, problem-solving, achievement-hungry ego that would love to map out and proceed smoothly along a straight and narrow path. The psyche's method is typically more labyrinthine. At the very least, the psyche will continue to invite people to crawl beneath their certainties and view the work from an underworld perspective. For most people, most of the time, this is not a comfortable posture.

Edward Edinger alludes to this uncomfortable position when he discusses the importance of maintaining a humble attitude toward the psyche. He interprets the beatitude "Blessed are the meek, for they shall inherit the earth" to mean that it is humility, not heroic striving for dominance, which ensures richness of the soul. A humble attitude, Edinger argues, "is fortunate because it is teachable and open to new considerations." The reward one earns is "an awareness of being individually related to . . . the wholeness of life." [100] Marie-Louise von Franz attests to the same principle in describing the goal of analytical work.

> We try to bring about a conscious attitude with which the person can keep the door to the unconscious open, which means that one must never be too sure of oneself, never be sure that what one says is the only possibility, never be too sure about a decision.
>
> One should always have an eye and an ear open towards the opposite, the other thing. That does not mean to be spineless, it doesn't mean just to sit there. It means to act according to one's conscious conviction, but still always having the humility to keep the door open and be proved wrong. [101]

Notice that von Franz makes an important point about conviction and decisiveness. One cannot simply abrogate responsibility by deciding not to decide or believing that this choice will do just as well as that, or any other. Developing and maintaining a good attitude toward the work requires taking a position, following a lead, drawing a line, and establishing a boundary. It also requires paying attention to the effects of such choices and being open to making a different choice if it becomes necessary.

An abiding allegiance to the psyche as a creative partner, which is first and foremost a matter of attitude, ensures a firsthand experience of the complexity and fluidity of psychological work. As the project takes shape, researchers will cycle through many phases including moments of insight, clarity and brilliance and moments of tedium, despair and frustration.

Clearly, some phases will be more welcome than others. The task is to accept them equally. Such an experience of the psyche's true complexity familiarizes people with a characteristic attributed to soul for millennia, at least since the contributions of Heraclitus in the sixth century B.C. That characteristic, says Thomas Moore, is movement.

> The presence of soul implies movement — not simply the ability to walk and run as Aristotle suggests, but an internal movement, a wandering and shifting of the soul itself. As the experience of life deepens and becomes focused in a wide variety of events engendering anything from joyful ecstasy to depressing pain, soul itself seems to move. From highs to lows, in depth and superficiality, vanishing into thin air or close to home, psychological vicissitudes can be felt as movements of soul. Soul even seems to travel through the body making its path traceable in a pounding heart, tingling nerves, or throbbing headache. We move through decision and action, and we are moved by passion and emotion.[102]

When the work seems stuck, one may need to pay closer attention to what is actually happening and look for subtle signs of movement. Perhaps the apparent stasis is one of the psyche's lures, inviting the inquiring person into a relationship of greater intimacy.

PERSONIFYING, PSYCHOLOGIZING, PATHOLOGIZING, AND DE-HUMANIZING

James Hillman's archetypal psychology derives primarily from that part of Jung's work that is founded on a strong commitment to the reality and autonomy of the psyche. He describes four moves that contribute, each in their own way, to this larger move of acknowledging psyche in the work. They are personifying, psychologizing, pathologizing, and de-humanizing, and we take them up here as specific practices related to welcoming the psyche.

Personifying should be somewhat familiar already as a move that forms the core of this book. In personifying, one relates to the psyche and all of the things, attitudes, and events of the world as though they were persons. This move invites the person to dwell within the animated world and acknowledge its aliveness and its soul. It relativizes the ego — that sense of a skin-encased separate personal identity that people carry and can get carried away with. Quite simply, a personified world is a living community characterized by lively engagements with other expressive persons at every turn. It should be obvious that conducting inquiry in a personified world will be very different than what most people encounter: the subjective personality wandering alone amidst a world full of dead, silent objects. Personifying is a move that will show up continually in the work, adding to its complexity and depth.

Psychologizing, or *seeing through*, is a familiar move as well. It begins with an attitude of anticipation and an assumption: once a person pays attention to the deeper layers of a phenomenon those layers will reveal themselves. Psychologizing is not meant to devalue the surfaces of the world. Instead, it is a way to see the surfaces as windows opening through to rich connections. Psychologizing instills the sense that the psyche resonates with its own stories and calls the person to hear them. People also encounter the wonderful paradox we referred to earlier, in Chapter 3, as the gap. As people see through the surfaces, they learn that the psyche hides as a way of inviting others to seek. The intention of seeing through layer upon layer is not to reach the bottom or the end, but to dance with the psyche as she moves, calling and receding, but never finishing.

Pathologizing is a less obvious move for most people. It rests on the assumption that the psyche is naturally inclined to see, or look for, what's wrong — even to make it up if necessary. Such is the case in perplexing dreams of people flying, butterflies swimming, and all manner of oppositions to acceptable reality. In Hillman's view the psyche is inclined toward derangement through the imagination. For some this idea may fly in the face of their idealization that the psyche is inclined toward balance and health. By acknowledging what is proven by common experience to be true — that the psyche uses the imagination to construct reality — Hillman obligates people to see the necessity of the pathological in any construct of balance or health.

Finally, the move Hillman calls *de-humanizing*, or soul-making, invites people to take human beings and human fantasies of dominion out of the central place in the psyche. It involves recognizing that Western culture is pervaded by what might be called dominion theology, in which the human, made in the image of God, occupies the central place in creation along with a right to control the rest of creation. In the world today, the best scientific and intellectual achievements are making it increasing clear that such dominion is both unlikely and undesirable, but humanity doesn't seem to know what to do about that. With the move of dehumanizing, the person begins to recognize, despite efforts to see it otherwise, that humans are only a part of the world and only a part of the psyche in the world. The world is ensouled through and through. Without recognizing this, relationship to the human soul becomes abstract and conceptual.

Taken as a whole these four moves — personifying, psychologizing, pathologizing, and de-humanizing — are some of the ways to acknowledge the reality of the psyche, Psyche's personhood. It is a practice of responding to her desire to be noticed, even as she moves into and out of the fields of awareness, and even as she presents paradoxes and challenges that seem to rob the person of the sense of power and control. Keeping these four moves in mind provides assurance of a strong partnership with the psyche. As we describe several other general moves, we will see how central this partnership is by how frequently aspects of this first move recur.

RITUAL

Ritual has a long history and venerable reputation, one that has been tarnished since the earliest days of what came to be known as the Enlightenment, when the belief in the power of humans to control their own fate reached its pitch. To this day, the fantasy of control is still widespread despite many reminders that "soul is closely connected to fate, and the turns of fate almost always go counter to the expectations and often to the desires of ego." It is simply "beyond our capacity to devise and to control."[103] Because the fantasy of control continues to exert its seductive pull, many believe ritual is an anachronism. Yet consider the way most people prepare themselves each morning for work: bathing, dressing in business clothes, eating breakfast, mulling over the day's schedule, and then setting out for the office. Those who do this Monday through Friday think of it as routine. Another name for it is ritual.

As the playwright David Mamet notes, the "supposed ability to side-step, to forgo, ritual comes from a mistaken belief in one's own powers and a misapprehension of personal grace. It is misplaced and it is sad, like the viewer at a magic show who analyzes the magician instead of enjoying the effect he creates."[104] One of the powers humanity has arrogated is the power to determine what is real and what is not. For the past 400 years or so, ritual has diminished in credibility because it suggests relationship to what cannot be measured, weighed, touched or seen — in other words, a relationship to what has no reality and therefore no worth. It is not that such things are unworthy of attention; there is nothing to attend to. Yet if attention is the cardinal psychological virtue and the task is to produce a psychological work, one must create ways to attend to the invisible and intangible psyche during the creative process. Rituals are concrete gestures that express the person's intention to devote the next hour, afternoon, or entire day to inquiry.

To speak from the perspective of soul, ritual is a way to acknowledge the psychic field as a lively, creative landscape that is peopled with autonomous images. Those engaged in psychological inquiry use ritual as a reminder that they are working within sacred space on behalf of wholeness both for themselves and for the opus. Ritual is also an excellent way to consciously create a container for the work.

Some of the ways that ritual appears in psychological inquiry are obvious, but they only become ritual when one does them intentionally. For example the space one works in, be it a studio, an office, or a study, can be just a space; or it can be a ritual space. How one makes it a ritual space can take many forms. These range from the simple, for instance lighting a candle to begin work, to the elaborate, which could include anything from choosing specific furnishings, symbolic artwork, and colors, to arranging the room according to the principles of *feng shui*. Other forms of ritual some of our students have used include setting aside specific hours or days for work and turning off the phone and ignoring e-mail during this time. Other students describe preparing a cup of tea or a glass of wine for themselves (and perhaps another for Psyche), placing fresh flowers in a vase, and burning incense. The content of the ritual itself does not matter as much as the commitment to honor one's participatory relationship with the psyche.

SEPARATION

A priest or shaman knows that taking off the vestments, the headdress, and the ornaments is as important in ending a ritual as putting them on is to begin ritual. Those engaged in psychological inquiry need to acknowledge separation from the work, too. Such separation establishes an important boundary between self and work, a boundary that is not always clear. Sometimes one becomes lost in such passionate connection with the work that it is all consuming and leaves no time for simple living. At others, the lack of apparent progress fosters a state of continual anxiety that affects every dimension of life, including leisure, without any respite. In either case, establishing boundaries is critical because it honors both the work and whatever else one values in life. Here there is a fortunate parallel to the work of psychotherapy as conceived by the Jungian analyst and writer, Adolf Guggenbühl-Craig. In his book *Power in the Helping Professions*, he points out the risks of depending on psychological work for connection to Eros. He makes it clear that there is a seductive aspect to working with the psyche that can tempt people to disengage from the rest of life with its more mundane forms of challenge. In doing so they may become involved with the shadow side of Eros by turning the work into an act of power and will. Guggenbühl-Craig makes equally clear that the simple remedy for this is to maintain connection to friends, family, and lovers, and to things of value outside of the work.[105]

Even for those who are psychologically inclined, not everything is psychological. In fact, in order to truly acknowledge what is psychological one must remember that psyche is a perspective, as discussed in the philosophical commitments of depth psychology, Chapter 3. The value of this perspective is derived, at least in part, from the fact that psyche is a *particular* perspective and only one of many needed for living. Therefore, one must become adept at not only entering it, but leaving it as well. When doing psychological work some things in life are better when they aren't part of the project.

TRANSFERENCE

One of the key themes of all approaches to inquiry that have developed
in the past century is an awareness of the relationship between observer
and observed, between researcher and topic, and between reader and
text. These, and numerous other examples, are corollaries to what had
previously been imagined as a sharp split between a perceiving subject
and the object of perception. That subject-object split has been soundly
discredited. In its place an array of tools has been developed that help one
perceive and establish the relational and participatory nature of inquiry.
The subject is no longer an object, but instead is an expressive, participating partner in acts of knowing. We have addressed this subject-object
split in Chapter 2 as it emerged historically in the evolution of qualitative
research. As it happens, the field of depth psychology has a long history of
working directly with a particular version of it.

Arising first in the realm of psychoanalytic theory, and particularly
with regard to the practice of psychoanalysis, Freud introduced the term
transference to describe a very concrete, if irrational, form of knowing that
assumes a fluid relationship between subject and object. Freud used the
term transference originally as a way of describing a patient's unconscious projection of difficult personal material onto others, particularly
the analyst, as a means of resisting analytic insight.[106] But as analysis of
the transference became the centerpiece of depth psychological practice,
the concept itself developed steadily into the awareness that transference
is really participation in a transferential field. Transference and projection are seen as descriptions of the natural exchange between knower and
known rather than some mistake one makes upon the other. Ultimately,
depth psychology asserts, they are the only means one has of knowing
anything at all. The fact that transference has been so thoroughly explored — at such a level of practical experience — by so many depth psychologists, makes a vast metaphorical context available to understand the
nature of knowing.

Jung scholar and phenomenologist Robert Romanyshyn has taken
this observation directly into the realm of research. Borrowing theory and
practice from Jung, he and his co-author Veronica Goodchild began developing what they call an imaginal approach to research using alchemical

hermeneutics as its primary method. Romanyshyn and Goodchild assume that the relationship between researcher and topic is one of transference — mutual transference. As such, it is a relationship that can be understood as parallel to the analytical relationship because it is called into being, developed, and fully realized by working through the transference.

A full account of Romanyshyn and Goodchild's approach to inquiry is soon to be published.[107] In it they refer to five guidelines or moves that reveal how body, heart, and soul are engaged in the transference, and therefore how a purely intellectual or academic approach to knowing will always fail to depict complex truths. Let's see how these five moves might emerge in the practice of reading a text.

First, the reader is asked to pay particular attention to how he or she is stopped by the text. In this moment, the forward motion of reading is halted by some spark between reader and text. Rather than label this moment as distraction, readers are encouraged to open to it as a meaningful shift in their relation to the text, and to see it as a matter coming from that relation. Being stopped, according to Romanyshyn and Goodchild, is "the moment when the researcher is being questioned by his or her topic, when the intentions of the reader are being 'stopped' by the soul of the work, by its 'intentions,' by what the topic wants from the researcher."[108]

Second, Romanyshyn and Goodchild ask readers to take this experience in through the body — to imagine an embodied connection between the body of the text and the body of the person. The point is to avoid conceptual or abstract interpretation of the moment. By requiring the experience to be held in the body, the way a dream is often remembered first as a physical sensation, readers stay in a related posture rather than adopting a reductive one.

> These moments of interruption are treated not just as a matter of mind; they are treated as matters of soul. The images, memories, or bodily felt sensations are not translated into abstractions. They are not made into concepts or ideas about oneself or the text. On the contrary, they are respectfully regarded as the animate and animating voice of the topic on its own terms, like one would treat a dream, for example.[109]

The third move asks the reader to suspend all traditional attempts to make sense of the text. In a curious reversal of Freud's earlier stance that the transference was a patient's resistance to insight, Romanyshyn and Goodchild suggests the apparent opposite — that attempted insight is a resistance to being caught up by the transference. Of course it is ultimately the same equation. The transference, if one can bear to stay with it, will reveal the deep erotic connections between text and reader. That in turn leads to a truer capacity to interpret and to represent whatever it is one has been called to study.

> If there is no getting around the fact that every act of interpretation is filtered through a complex, then the radical choice that we face as researchers is whether we do our work with or without awareness of their presence and effects. Working out these complex relations in the transference dialogues is a procedural way, then, of being responsible for the body of work that one produces. [110]

The fourth move is aimed at revealing the different layers of the transference ranging from the personal level to the cultural historical level. The personal level is revealed by examples of misreading the text reminiscent of the way Jung discovered the role of the complexes by studying "errors" in his word association experiments. The cultural historical transference is revealed by examples of interpretive bias. In this moment, reflective attention helps readers distinguish between the levels, since they might otherwise remain unconscious.

The fifth move calls for the silent reader to become a vocal one — to read aloud. Romanyshyn and Goodchild suggest that this move inclines the reader toward reverie, which is an opening to the imaginal layer within the text. This also gives knowing its body and breath.

> This amplification seeks to attend to research not only in terms of the ego mind and its literate bias, but also in terms of the vocal soul and its oral bias. The challenge here is to develop a mode of writing that attends to both biases, to a way of writing down the soul, which is as beautiful, emotional, and seductive as it is true, thoughtful, and educational.

The implications of applying the notion of transference to inquiry are significant. Romanyshyn and Goodchild's work is an ongoing exploration of how this psychological phenomenon becomes a most effective tool in remedying the myth of objectivity, one part of the distorted view of the world that has been passed down in the Western tradition.

As a note of caution, although psychological inquiry can be a joy, it is unusually demanding. It asks one *to be fully involved with the opus on every level*. This kind of inquiry is not merely an intellectual exercise. It obligates the person to participate intellectually, emotionally, imaginatively, spiritually, and physically, because the work extends well beyond the ego to reverberate in the depths of the soul. At these deeper levels, the work truly becomes psychological, unearthing wounds and complexes that otherwise may have remained unconscious. Confronting these complexes can stop the work far more emphatically than a mere intellectual juggernaut can. At times, simple perseverance will be an act of personal courage. Many who have done this kind of work have realized at some point that they were engaging in soul retrieval. That is, their work integrated aspects of the personal psyche to restore their individual health, and it integrated aspects of the objective psyche to enhance humanity's collective wisdom. The personal and archetypal nature of psychological inquiry makes the work especially meaningful and especially arduous.

DIALOGUE

Dialogue, as defined by the physicist David Bohm, is the practice of sitting with a small group of people who dedicate themselves to the meaning that arises within the group in the present moment. It requires a skillful balance of the personal and the communal and careful attention to what is both spoken and not spoken. One of the greatest challenges in dialogue is not rehearsing what one is going to say before another person has finished speaking. Another is to carefully judge, before speaking, whether what one needs to say will be a contribution to the group. Bohm explains that the name "dialogue" comes from two Latin words, "dia" (*through*) and "logos" (*meaning*).[111] In dialogue the intention is to follow meaning as it winds its way through the process. No one leads and there is no agenda.

Instead, people allow ideas present themselves and follow their connections, listen to all of the voices without taking sides, and hear every
contribution as a distinctive expression of the complex, multi-faceted
psyche. Dialogue requires listening into the depths of the silences while
paying attention to the discomfort this produces and noting the common
assumption that nothing is happening. In dialogue, one relinquishes control and practices the patient, attentive receptivity that we have called the
yin of inquiry.

The praxis of dialogue requires a rare and exceptional skill, emotional
wisdom. Emotional wisdom combines an awareness of emotion with re-
straint and reflection so that people can choose how, when, and where
to express themselves. Emotional wisdom is especially necessary when a
person is engaged in a creative project whose worth depends upon receptivity. Whether one is in dialogue with human beings, with texts, or with
phenomena in the more-than-human world, open, vulnerable participation with others can rouse surprising, complex, and confusing feelings.
"Emotion is the body, concrete and visible, here and now," notes James
Hillman. "The more body in an event, the more emotion." Furthermore,
emotion requires people to "live in the bonds of this very moment, the
time just exactly as it is," presenting them with the concrete precision of
their existence, "painful and ugly as it can be at times."[112] As the will is
frustrated, people become aware of conflict and disorder. They gain profound insight into the complexity and multiplicity of the personal psyche,
which is a valuable corrective to any single-minded, simplifying attitude.

Instead of rising above the pain, ugliness, and chaos of concrete existence, the practice of dialogue challenges people to attend to such emotions. In light of the importance of the symptom as the soul's mode of
expressing itself, engaging in a dialogue with unwelcome emotions — and
the phenomena that arouse them — is a meaningful way to attend to the
psyche. It takes courage to participate in the creative process with this degree of openness, but anything less does not serve or support psychological inquiry. Whatever ideas people may have about remaining unmoved,
detached, and in control of the work quickly dissolve because emotion
causes them to fall into the ancestral past and into the flesh. People also
fall into what they most cares about, which includes deep, abiding values
and cherished beliefs.

The practice of dialogue, as we have said, need not be limited to conversation with human beings. One of our students, Craig Chalquist, developed a method for dialogue with the spirit of place — in Latin the *genius loci* — which he named *locianalysis*. His extensive fieldwork at each of California's mission towns and the modern cities that grew up around them revealed persistent, traumatic themes. Deep, embodied listening to these places sparked strong personal emotions, which he welcomed and integrated into his research. His work, in its own uniquely moving way, asked the three questions native to the inquisitive psyche: Who's here? What's wrong? What does it mean? His literal journey along California's mission trail and his symbolic journey into the heart of these wounded places also led him to the core of his own wounds. He discovered that place and person are inextricably intertwined; peace is impossible if one's homeland is in agony.[113]

Paradoxically, the fall into emotion, which is a personal experience, reunites people with what is universally human or archetypal. *One moves by way of the personal to the archetypal.* Thus, deeply attending to emotion in the practice of dialogue is an entry into the personal psyche and the more-than-personal psyche. The relationship with the psyche becomes profound, intimate and rich, guiding the formation of the work and the transformation of the worker.

COLLABORATION AND ISOLATION

In the spirit of the philosophical commitment to the dialectical psyche we have placed this pair of moves, collaboration and isolation, side by side. The intention is to portray them as corresponding qualities or sensibilities, not opposites, meaning that in the course of psychological inquiry one calls for the other. By collaboration we mean intentional opening to otherness, for example, by finding scholars who clearly have adopted a different perspective on the topic or by listening assiduously to co-researchers whose ideas or attitudes are surprising, startling, and even challenging. Collaboration is related to dialogue, as described previously, but is a broader move that includes a cultivated sense of participation in the larger field, as well as a relativization of the working ego. It is seeing one's self as a part of the inquiry and not its focal point or even its sole author. If this move isn't undertaken somewhere along the way, thinking will be unconsciously reductive and intellectually narcissistic.

One reason collaboration is so important is that thinking and writing are activities that favor logic, clarity, and consistency. This is not a problem in itself, but it also happens that one of the easiest ways to be clear and consistent is to echo the familiar — to gain authority from old ideas by restating them. Researchers thus become subscribed to established intellectual discourse in order to provide an authoritative medium for their explorations. But if this is the case how can the work represent the multiplicity and complexity of the psyche? In reflecting on their project, how can researchers evaluate, or even grasp, the perspectival nature of what they have so lovingly focused upon in such a personal way? John Rowan, who writes about what he and others have called *new paradigm research*, says

> It is increasingly clear that there are many different ways of being in this world, many levels of awareness about alternative 'spaces' that we may occupy either permanently or temporarily, but the trouble is that we have few clear or shared ways of identifying these or of talking about them. [114]

One way to address this problem is to consciously strive for collaboration. But what is collaboration, and what is this otherness one seeks to include?

The most obvious form of collaboration in research is given in methods that mandate a substantial and ongoing participation with the persons or communities being studied. There are many new approaches to qualitative research that take this as their starting point. Some even include the co-researchers in the formative stages of the work, such as developing a research concern or question. Even large groups of participating co-researchers, however, can unconsciously move toward single-minded, consensual thinking. Thus it is possible to literalize collaboration by adopting strategies and structures for inclusion but still miss the point.

Collaboration, in psychological terms, means opening to difference. Researchers allow themselves to be impacted through engagement with an *other*, an engagement that they may want to resist or ignore at first.

As such, collaboration often feels difficult, challenging, even disorienting. It can appear to interrupt the work or, at the least, be inconvenient.

Collaboration, as a move in psychological inquiry, requires researchers to treat disturbance as a positive thing. It is a reminder that some matters of interest and some perspectives have not yet been included. This opening to alternative perspectives is necessary to assure that the work is spacious enough for the psyche to move about in. As John Rowan says, "once we allow ourselves to see that there are alternatives to traditional ways of thinking and being in [the] world, we may permit ourselves to search for, explore, and practice them." [115] As an attitude of opening toward otherness, collaboration extends throughout the project of inquiry. In a scholarly work it will affect the way researchers construct the topic, approach the literature, assemble participants and mentors, gather and analyze data, and in the way they write.

The move of collaboration is complemented by isolation. No matter how inclusive researchers hope to be in terms of interests, perspectives, and goals, there are points along the way where they must make decisions about what belongs to the work and what does not in order to proceed. Remaining open to assure inclusiveness and spaciousness is clearly necessary, yet it must be balanced by limits and boundaries. At various points in the process, researchers must pull all the interests, voices, attitudes, goals, and fears into a room of sorts and close the door. Once inside, the alchemical processes of inquiry can begin. In fact the metaphor of alchemy suggests an appropriate image: the hermetic jar into which the materials of the work are placed and sealed so that Hermes can do his work.

In developing his research method called *heuristics*, Clark Moustakas offers the term *indwelling*, which we find useful in thinking about isolation as a move in psychological inquiry.

> Indwelling refers to the heuristic process of turning inward to seek a deeper, more extended comprehension of the nature or meaning of a quality or theme of human experience. It involves a willingness to gaze with unwavering attention and concentration into some fact of human experience in order to understand its constituent qualities and its wholeness. [116]

In actual practice most projects of inquiry are already characterized by a high degree of isolation. Anyone who was written a book, a thesis, or a dissertation will recall those times when they stopped reading, closed the door, turned off the phone, and went into the hermetic jar to think, reflect, and to write. Even if the work is a group project there will be a turning inward in order to reflect and to produce. But by placing the idea of isolation in dialogue with its partner, collaboration, we are encouraging conscious awareness of the back and forth movement between them so that researchers can feel their place in the continuum all along the way.

PRESENTATION AND REPRESENTATION

The moves of presentation and representation involve consciously taking on the role of speaker for the ideas, images, and hopes of the project. Researchers must ask themselves two equally important questions, "Who is speaking?" and "Who am I speaking for?" These moves also address the hidden strategies involved in the act of presentation as well as the psychological, social, and political issues inherent in acts of representation. The larger goal, simply, is to bring awareness of these issues into the process of psychological inquiry and the production of the final work.

The voice of presentation is often given by the field into which the presentation is made. For example, in most cases scholarly presentation demands a voice that is insightful, erudite, eloquent, and clear. On the other hand poetic presentation tends to be imagistic, metaphorical, lyric, and embodied. Science prefers a factual, precise, completed presentation that is not open to multiple understandings. Of course, there are many more modes of presentation, and one could break each of these down further. Researchers may begin by asking such questions as "Whose voice will I be taking up, and why?" and "What impression am I hoping or intending to create by adopting this voice?" It is not possible to present anything without adopting some mode of presentation, so it will not be enough to skirt this concern by saying, "I will just be myself and let the work stand for itself." Researchers must go more deeply into it.

Sometimes working through this question of presentation, the identity of the speaker, is an act of personal transformation. For example, one student made a very powerful, even psychoactive connection to her field of interest. She found herself engaging the questions in the work with a deep sense of adventure and a lot of creative enthusiasm. But when she tried to write she found the work to be less interesting — even going dead. Moving back and forth between these opposing attitudes she began to feel a lot of despair about the project and began to consider giving up on it. Fortunately she was able to see that the problem occurred with writing. With this insight, she realized the voice she was using was stilted, critical, and fatherly, tending to judge the material as its main mode of presentation. For many years this was the voice that she had adopted when doing scholarly work. She had never questioned it because she never realized there was a choice. Once she had seen this it was not difficult to begin playing with a new mode of presentation. She found that it was not necessary to adopt the voice of the *father* to write in the voice of the *scholar*. It was a transformative realization in that she has never gone back to the old mode of presentation.

In addition to how researchers present the work, there is the problem of whom they purport to represent and what the overall implications are. We briefly addressed this concern within the larger field of qualitative research in Chapter 2, where it has been called a crisis of representation. The concern doesn't represent a crisis so much as an opportunity to see the work in yet another rich layer of context. It allows researchers to reconsider the ethical questions living in the field of study and recreated in their particular piece of it.

The political concern about representation can be stated quite simply, thanks to a few decades of agonizing debate and self examination in the realms of social science. Knowledge is power, and power is used both for and against people, communities, and cultures. Academic and institutionally derived knowledge has been privileged over indigenous and locally derived knowledge, consistently damaging some interests in the local setting. Critical awareness of this privilege and its effects has led to the legitimate questioning of researchers' authority to represent the experience of others. Simply put, what gives someone a right to occupy a place of power that includes exercising the authority of representation? How is the person using or abusing that power? Responsible researchers must account for the implicit power relationships existing in the realm of scholarship and in practices of research.

Beyond the ways that representation has been addressed as a political issue, it is a central concern in psychological inquiry for one simple reason: researchers are representing the psyche. As we stated in Chapter 3, the psyche is both personal and more than personal. Although one's only authoritative experience of the psyche is given at the personal level, one is both inclined and called upon to represent this personal experience as comprehensive and universal. This is a difficult tension to hold and we have no formulaic remedy for it. One way to work with the tension is simple awareness. Researchers can periodically examine how they take on the authority of representation.

More than once, students have reached the end of a project burdened with a profound sense of failure regarding the issue of representation. In one case a man ended up redoing his fieldwork, which involved an additional 3 months of effort, because he did not see how radically he was misrepresenting the situation in the field until he read his own words. There is no perfect solution for this concern, partly because presenting findings and representing experience are, to some degree, always fictional in the sense that researchers produce a narrative, or story. However, beginning the inquiry with an awareness of the challenge is far better than having a surprise at the end.

Concerns about presentation and representation need to be addressed not only as researchers do their own writing but in their reading as well. Researchers may ask themselves "Which authors am I collaborating with and why do I choose them?" and "What are their sources of authority?" Such questions are certainly critical, but they do not inevitably devalue the representation. Rather they provide a context for interpretation and thereby make the knowledge gained more useful.

LANGUAGE

One's relationship to language — regardless of whether one is working in or out of the field of psychology — is important from the beginning of the project through to the end. Language and words[117] are the milieu of the inquiring mind. As such they can easily be forgotten in the same way a fish forgets about water. Because depth psychology aims to remember what is forgotten, it makes a rich and interesting contribution, giving language its due. Thus, closely related to both presentation and representation is another collection of important moves that focus on language.

The overwhelming attitude toward language and words is one of correctness, utility, and clarity. The central move one makes with language in psychological inquiry involves a profound shift in attitude. Instead of regarding it as a tool for communication and explication, one thinks of language as a living being and a co-participant in the work. Such a shift in attitude restrains people from attempting to master and use language for the purposes of clear exposition in speaking and writing. It becomes apparent that language, as a living being, is capable of constructing reality on its own. Moreover, it is quite capable of using people.

Hillman offers an example of the power of language in psychotherapy, where he describes its ability to create soul in the clinical setting. His words can just as easily apply to the art of inquiry.

> The overwhelming difficulty of communicating soul in talk becomes crushingly real when two persons sit in two chairs, face to face and knee to knee, as in an analysis with Jung. Then we realize what a miracle it is to find the right words, words that carry soul accurately, where thought, image and feeling interweave. Then we realize that soul can be made on the spot simply through speech. Such talk is the most complex psychic endeavor imaginable.[118]

In *The Myth of Analysis*, Hillman says that the work of psychology should aim to rectify language by recognizing the tendency to use words in deadening ways — something he finds particularly problematic in the field of psychology.[119] If people began to see words as living beings instead of dead things, wouldn't they have to hold the work differently from the outset? Once people are willing to acknowledge this possibility a whole host of moves present themselves as ways to enliven the work.

One of the most fascinating ways that language shows itself to be alive is in the realm of mistakes. Freud's essay on slips of the tongue[120] and Jung's word association experiments[121] both recognized that apparent mistakes represent a kind of direct linkage between language and the unconscious and as such can serve as portals to a wild landscape of thought, image, and experience. Mistakes one makes with words — whether they happen in reading, writing, or speaking — are direct connections to the psyche and potential veins of gold one can explore for meaning beyond the surface. If this is true it invites a whole new approach to editing. Of course basic editing requires researchers to ultimately correct all errors in spelling, meaning, and grammar. But in light of this possibility one might first take note of each mistake, imagining it as a possible window into something that wants to be seen. It could be about the topic, or the researcher, or about the language itself doing its work. Even if most cases prove to be worthless mistakes, slowing down to pay attention to them places researchers in a more engaged relationship with psyche's wildness.

For example, a student recalled doing a spell check correction on a poem she had transcribed. The word in question should have been written *defloration* but showed up as *deploration*. She paused long enough before correcting the spelling to research the word defloration and found countless examples of deplorable acts associated with it. These images became engaged with her interpretive reading of the poem adding a richness that would not have been attempted otherwise.

Another language-related move is to pay particular attention to words with questionable meanings. If a word presents itself as enigmatic, it may be a good time to study it. Or perhaps one wants to use a word that is not altogether familiar. In such a moment, researchers could imagine that the word is reaching for them as much as the other way round. Studying the word could take researchers to the dictionary, which is good; but why stop there? How about the Thesaurus? Even better, researchers could use a dictionary of etymology and explore the life of this word and its immediate ancestors. More times than not this research into words themselves enriches the prefabricated landscapes of thought found in established discourse.

One area of particular concern is the tendency in academic writing to use words that take the place of meaning rather than making meaning. This is difficult to assess. After all, don't all words attempting to envelop and convey extensive meanings in a clear and concise way? Yes, they do.

Over time, however, that may lead to deadness. It happens like this. Some words that come into use are so successful at conveying meaning that they gobble up larger and larger portions of it until they reach a point where they bloated and indistinct. They have tried to mean so much that they no longer really mean anything at all. That is when they die and should be laid to rest. But often that is also just when they are picked up in popular culture and used and abused until they are nothing but the breath one uses to say them. The word *patriarchy* is a good example of this. It is a word that originally brought about a provocative reevaluation of cultural values that had been unconsciously biased toward a masculine perspective. It has been so successful at inserting itself into so many levels of so many contexts that it is now being used as a kind of shorthand for all that is bad in contemporary Western culture. It is a dead word because to use it thoughtfully these days one is required to define it in context. If so, then one might as well simply let the words of definition carry the meaning since the word itself might buckle under the stress.

Most psychological language is quite dead in part because people have asked words to do their thinking for them — to carry too much meaning. But this problem can occur in any field of interest. The remedy is a simple one. It is to notice one's tendency to use big words and to carefully examine what one is asking of them. Unpack their bags a bit and see if there is a way to restore their capacity to inspire the imagination. It is one's job to make meaning by playing with words, not by making them do all the work. For example, with the word *patriarchy*, researchers might explore its deeper meanings before using it. What are its core meanings, its nuances, and most importantly, its images? How might researchers be stretching the word *patriarchy* in the current context and what are possible alternative phrases, words, or narratives? If words and images prefer to be related erotically — that is they desire one another — then what images might a word long for and how can one provide it?

In early Renaissance painting important communications were often depicted by little winged angels, or Erotes, leaving the mouth of a speaking figure and entering the ear of the listener. This is a different picture of language and words, revealing their sacredness, power, and eroticism. If psychological inquiry seeks to represent the deeper and more complex aspects of the world, this is the image of language and words that it needs. It is a very complex endeavor but it begins with a simple shift in attitude.

There are many other moves of language, some we have mentioned and others we will explore in the next chapter. In closing we want to re-call the problem of representation from the previous section and look at it in the context of language and words. We want to encourage research-ers to think about all the complex phenomena they are obligated to rep-resent and begin to see words and language as willing participants in that work. When one invites the psyche into the work, one is at the same time inviting the logos or the words of the psyche into the work. They are not dead objects.

5

APPLYING THE MOVES OF PSYCHOLOGICAL INQUIRY TO SCHOLARLY RESEARCH

Scholarly research conducted within or guided by academic institutions is a formal undertaking that tends to follow a fairly consistent sequence of stages. This is true regardless of the work's final form: thesis, dissertation, or book. In fact, authors of books written outside the purview of academia also tend to see their work through this same series of stages, beginning with developing a preliminary idea of the research through finalizing the manuscript. Familiarity with these stages gives researchers a sense of the individual parts that make up the whole project. It's a structure that can be helpful in transforming a formidable task into a manageable one. In this chapter, we identify five discrete stages of research:

- Stage 1: developing a preliminary idea of the project
- Stage 2: beginning background reading and exploratory research
- Stage 3: moving from topic to inquiry
- Stage 4: extending the research
- Stage 5: completing the research

When one actually enters each stage of research instead of simply thinking about it, its unique challenges and demands become clear. The work begins to take physical shape in the form of piles of books and journals, research notes, phone calls and email with key participants, travel to research sites, collections of artifacts, interview transcripts, exploratory writing, a steadily growing bibliography, and chapter drafts. Especially in the first few stages of the research, individuals reflect upon and negotiate the distance between all that they hoped to do and what they actually *can* do. Each stage presents opportunities to ground the work in the depth psychological perspective with the result that the reality of the psyche shifts from an interesting philosophical idea to a daily experience. Researchers learn firsthand what an active, autonomous, inspiring, maddening, and playful co-author Psyche truly is.

This chapter describes the five stages of the work in practical terms. It suggests some of the specific ways to apply the moves of psychological inquiry described in Chapter 4. We also suggest additional moves that make sense in particular moments of the research process. We have adopted a slightly different mode for this which includes taking a number of questions we have been asked by students over the years and providing answers that have helped to move the work forward.

STAGE I: DEVELOPING A PRELIMINARY IDEA

We have said that the art of inquiry obligates the individual to be centered in and on the psyche from the moment the work begins until it ends. Yet the life of a creative work often has mysterious beginnings. Moreover, who can know with certainty when it ends? Concepts such as the beginning and the end are fictional constructs, ego decisions, or both. People use them because they're handy, they work as part of the story, and because they help create a useful container for the work — not because they are literally true. In fact nowhere is the profound depth of inquiry felt so keenly as in the first task the researcher faces: developing a preliminary idea of the topic. Selecting a theme, premise, or focus is difficult for any writer. Continuing to make good choices so that the material supports the selected theme is another challenge. This is partly why a potentially brilliant work — regardless of whether it's a three-page essay or a 300-page dissertation — can end up completely banal.

Developing a preliminary idea presents an additional difficulty, however, which is this: Such research is a vocation that reflects, even if unconsciously, an authentic longing that can only be satisfied by a particular piece of work. Responding to vocation is not wholly an ego decision. It requires paying attention to hints from the psyche, which can include flashes of intuition and deep movements of desire, then allowing time to respond to them. Psyche *and* eros are both present in the decision to do a particular piece of research. For many people, the choice unfolds organically. Often there is an "oh, of course!" quality to it. This is not to say that there is only one kind of work that calls to the person or that there won't be other callings at other times. The distinguishing feature of any particular vocation, however, is that it appears in one time and place. It is the person's creative response to the vocation that makes the work entirely unique.

The subject of vocation is often mentioned in religious contexts because the idea of something mysterious inviting or compelling one to undertake a task seems vaguely religious. Jung realized that the whole process of encountering the psyche "is quintessentially religious, a true vocation, because heeding the 'inner voice' brings revelation."[122] But Jung was not the first. Others, including Heraclitus, Socrates, and Plato, whom we have already discussed, were quite clear that placing the psyche at the center of a work or a life is a religious endeavor. This classical idea, which went underground or was transformed for nearly two millennia, reappears in the work of the fifteenth-century neo-Platonist Marsilio Ficino. Ficino "found soul to be the proper mediating factor in all his studies — in philosophy and theology, in medicine and psychotherapy, and in his religious devotion."[123] In discussing this idea, Thomas Moore affirms Ficino's belief and describes its relevance for humanity today.

> There is indeed a relationship between soul and religion, between psychology and religious awareness; for without soulful fantasy all is profane and secular, a world reduced to serve as fodder for our pragmatic intentions. With soul comes an intense sense of value, an ordering of desires, and a respect for common things because they have such impact on the human spirit.[124]

The preliminary idea for a work may grow out of an intense sense of value or it may lead to an intense restructuring of the person's values. Sometimes it does both. The point is that vocation carries deep levels of meaning that the person may never come to know.

The idea of vocation may be enticing, but there's a practical issue to address. How exactly does one hear a call? Two of the techniques discussed in the previous chapter are relevant at this time: adopting a receptive attitude and extending hospitality to the images and ideas that spontaneously appear. It is also important to pay attention to every cue, intellectual, emotional, physical, and imaginal, because any or all of these can lead to an area of interest. Especially at this time, one should not discount the value of a strong intuition. And one should follow it, which is another way of saying, *allow it to lead*. For example, if you come across an intriguing paragraph in a book, read more. Or if someone makes an interesting comment, write it down. If a play, film, or work of art is disturbing or provocative, go see it again, note it in a journal, talk it over with a friend. One student spent an entire weekend reading through every paper she had written while doing her doctoral coursework, noting the themes and questions she returned to again and again. From this, she had the starting point for her project.

One very important resource for this stage of the work is one's dream life. Dreams will often participate quite actively in creative work. Many of our students have had the experience of their topic first appearing to them, complete with the title, in the midst of a dream. Other students have invited their dreams to comment on important decisions. One way to do this is to make a choice, that is, take an ego position, and then watch what the dream has to say.

Two questions that are helpful at this stage of the research include "What fascinates me or compels my attention?" and "What image, issue or idea won't leave me alone?" The second question reflects a common experience, which is that often there is a nagging quality to vocation. Some guests have to knock repeatedly at the door to be allowed in. At other times, particular emotional cues signal vocation. For instance, what issue or idea inspires eagerness, delight, fury, or indignation? By attending to these, a preliminary idea for the research is often very close at hand. The prolific author Ray Bradbury describes the essential role of emotion in fueling the creative quest. He says "if you are writing without zest, without gusto, without love, without fun, you are only half a writer," then goes on to add that "the first thing a writer should be is — excited. He should be a thing of fevers and enthusiasms. Without such vigor he might as well be out picking peaches or digging ditches; God knows it'd be better for his health."[125]

The active receptivity needed for approaching research work as a vocation may be very uncomfortable for individuals who are accustomed to thinking swiftly and decisively. So too, the intense emotions that sometimes mark vocational work can feel disconcerting or unmanageable. It may be helpful to remember that the way of psyche is labyrinthine rather than linear. Getting lost is part of the journey. In trying to find an area of interest, one is likely to flail about for awhile, confused and uncertain or even feverish. If this happens be kind to yourself. Allow your mind to wander and wonder.

My problem has been that I really have too many topics and I can't decide which one to pursue.

The move of personifying can help one imagine the initial engagement with possible topics in a very animated way. See the topic as a person coming to play, maybe even bringing with it some surprise guests. Soon the room and your mind can become scattered, disorganized, and uncertain. You may find yourself exhausted by the possibilities. But to think of it in this way also allows a space for inner dialogues to begin. Allow the possibilities to address one another. Ask them to describe their intentions for you and the work. Pay attention to each competing voice as though you might be a teacher in a vibrant classroom.

This chaotic and disorganized moment is very common in the phase of developing a preliminary idea and it is also quite consistent with the psyche's tendency to give value to all that shows up. The challenge is to stay open, remember that chaos is normal, and gradually listen for the inner dialogues to begin organizing themselves. In this process you might find it helpful to keep a project journal so that you have a place for all your ideas to take preliminary shape. Read through it on occasion and reflect. Another aid some have found useful is to create a picture of this chaos and chart its movements. On a large piece of paper draw a circle and then pin up all the ideas, topics, and subtopics that seem to want to play. Then move them around as intuition and attention guide you. In one project Joe used this process to discover that an idea he originally thought was central to the topic was, in fact, more of a muse. The idea only wanted to be an active witness or commentator and had no strong desire to be written about. This became clear when one day it simply migrated out of the circle but remained on the paper.

My problem is that I don't feel inspired by any of the ideas that present themselves. Most of the time nothing presents at all.

This could happen for a variety of reasons. For example, it may come up in situations where one is required to do the project but just doesn't feel ready. Some reasons for this could be fatigue, boredom, or even fear. In any case, since what seems painfully missing is a capacity for imagination, we suggest bringing the imagination into the problem. You are being stopped. What are the images (emptiness, denseness, deadness, etc.) of that stopping? Allow the images to comment on your situation and your project. You might also consider what other thing seems to hold your attention instead. Focusing on the stopping brings some movement into the process of inquiry. It is that movement which makes space for something necessary, if unexpected, to show. Of course it is always possible that you find yourself at a time and place where doing a project of research just isn't your soul's calling. In which case, take a break from it all.

The idea of a calling is a bit mystical to me. How do I know when I am the one being called?

This is a wonderful and intensely psychological question. Its importance obviously extends far beyond the confines of the project of inquiry, and as such it points to how psychological inquiry can serve the deepest needs of the soul. It is, therefore, not an easily answered question.

In our experience a calling from the soul comes as a mixed blessing — like good news and bad news. So it ought to evoke some strong ambivalence. It might feel like a challenge that you dread and at the same time one you have longed for. It might be helpful to contrast the feeling of being called with its opposite which would be the urge to do a project that simply meets the requirement, feels safe and manageable. Another way of describing a personal calling is that it feels haunted. There are ghosts there — spirits demanding their remembrance. They may be personal ghosts, cultural or racial ghosts, or ghosts of other callings un-heeded, but there would be a sense of being haunted. This is an example of the transference discussed in Chapter 4. Perhaps the most important sign of a calling, at least for the art of inquiry, is the sense of the unknown mixed with a desire to know. This is essential to psychological inquiry — particularly when one gets to the stage of formulating a question. You will know it by the feel of anxious curiosity. You will become a seeker.

STAGE 2: BACKGROUND READING AND PREPARATORY RESEARCH

Once the researcher has found a preliminary idea — or it has found the researcher — it's helpful to imagine the area of research as a landscape. This landscape is alien at first, but it will slowly become familiar through reading, reflection, and writing. After exploring for a bit, the researcher may jump over one landscape entirely and find another. Eventually the researcher will be forced to stake a claim to the territory. Even then, a clear premise or specific question may not present itself. That's okay. If exploring this area is truly a vocational undertaking, the researcher will quickly face the problem of selecting one premise or idea among a fertile abundance of them.

At this stage of the research, it is important to begin compiling a list of references. One way to do this is to scavenge the footnotes, endnotes, and bibliographies of books that are particularly rich or appealing; these provide important resources for additional reading. Also pay attention to provocative and intriguing statements and jot down your initial response to them. Perhaps these statements express your belief better than you could have yourself. Perhaps you strongly disagree. In any event, where you respond, take note. This is the material that carries weight, and can carry the research forward.

It is sometimes helpful to imagine this phase of the work as one of gathering, sifting, and sorting. Many researchers have had moments where they have wished they could just shift their priorities for a time and really dig into some particular interest. Most often, unless one makes a conscious choice, such moments pass unnoticed. Psychological inquiry will involve a decision to reset priorities and engage the field of interest with passion and devotion.

I feel like I have been reading about this topic forever and want to just get on with writing at this point.

You may very well have a deep familiarity with the literature given your long term interest in the topic, but it will be important to reanimate this literary landscape by entering with as much of a naive mind as possible. Use your deeper understanding of how you have been called to the topic to acknowledge your transference to the various ideas and their authors. Use that investigation to re-read the material more deeply. You should be concerned if you have chosen a topic that no longer interests you enough to read further. That being said, it is often the case that the best rhythms are achieved when one does the deep reading and the reflective and interpretive writing in the same time frame. You may be in such a situation so that what feels like a disinterest in reading is actually a sense of urgency to begin writing. Doing both together could work.

It's been easy for me to immerse myself in research, and I have extensive notes, but I seem to freeze up when I try to write anything worthwhile.

The first thing to point out in this sort of problem is that doing research is not only writing. Research almost always includes extensive reading and note taking and can include interviewing people and observing situations, places, or things. While some writing does occur during research — for instance, refining a set of interview questions or summarizing an author's position — it is not yet the creative writing that all authors must do to produce a finished work. So though you are immersing yourself in the project and making good progress, doing research doesn't prepare you for the task of writing. It's like training for a marathon by going for a three-mile walk every day. After a year or so you'll be a great walker but you won't be a marathon runner.

One way to prepare yourself to write a lengthy work is to begin exercising your writing muscle early in the project. On the days you set aside for research, plan to spend a set number of minutes of that time writing. Don't worry about how many pages you produce. Don't worry about whether or not the writing is good enough for the final manuscript. Don't worry about whether or not it sounds right or reflects your authentic voice. Don't even worry about whether or not the ideas are worthwhile, weighty, or truly original. That voice and those ideas will come, eventually. Your only goal is to write.

One technique that has worked for some students is to get yourself an old-fashioned kitchen timer — one that audibly ticks — set it for an amount of time you choose, and simply start. When the timer goes off, stop. Whether you're in mid-sentence, mid-paragraph, or mid-idea, stop. There are a few strong reasons for this. First, stopping in middle will make you hungry to write again. Second, the ideas will continue to dance in your imagination and perhaps show up in your dreams, growing and maturing on their own between writing sessions. Third, each time you sit down to write you are likely to feel a burst of energy and enthusiasm, particularly if you adopt a playful attitude towards beating the clock. The fact is, people tend to place a high value on scarce commodities, and by limiting your writing time you are raising its value. Sure, it's a trick. But it works. You'll be surprised how quickly a few good pages a week adds up, transforming a huge writing task into a surprisingly joyful and manageable project.

Perhaps the most important outcome of the regular writing sessions is that they foster what we call *ecology of creativity*. In healthy ecosystems, substances move. In Chapter 3 we spoke at length about the fluid psyche. So let us imagine, for a moment, an ecological understanding of the dynamic creative process. Research is the inflow of information. Writing is outflow. If you immerse yourself in research without writing, you are creating a stoppage in the creative process. Writing even for a short time every day enhances the dynamic play of ideas, giving them the time and space they need to mature into understanding and wisdom.

Every time I go to the library I find myself reading things that take the topic in a different direction. I feel like I am getting more confused about what I am trying to do.

This is a delicate sort of problem. In fact it is important not to label it as a problem too quickly. At this stage of the work the preliminary idea and the preliminary work with the literature are often happening simultaneously, and require the willingness to wander and digress. However this can also be a sign of resistance that expresses unconscious ambivalence about the project.

We suggest that you create a structure for this experience. Spend at least some of your time reading a work that is clearly on topic, as you have already defined it. When you feel your reading choices moving in another direction, try to identify that direction by naming it. Put that direction into a kind of dialogue with the original one and see what comes from that.

Remember that one good reason for background reading is that it establishes the literary landscape. As such, some of your reading will be closer to the central idea and other reading will be more peripheral. There also will be reading that is ultimately beyond the bounds of the inquiry, but you can't know this until you have spent time in that part of the landscape.

STAGE 3: MOVING FROM TOPIC TO INQUIRY

Although inquiry is a natural activity of the psyche, achieving and holding an attitude of inquiry is not necessarily a simple task. Your project can easily become stuck at the beginning through an inability to distinguish between a topic of interest and a matter for inquiry. They are very different and have different roles in the work.

A topic is a theme or field of interest. There are many reasons why researchers align themselves with a topic, including some that are decidedly not inquiring. It may be inherited the way one might inherit a religion or political affiliation from parents or cherished teachers. Researchers can become identified with a topic because of some previous success with it, and then choose to stay with the feel of that success. Some topics actually protect people from thinking and from vulnerability to the change that a new one might bring. Some topics are overly grand, almost cosmological, and they hold sway because they are too grand to question. It is unlikely that they will engender a lively and critical inquiry. Not, that is, unless researchers consciously and intentionally shift toward a more inquiring relationship to the topic.

As you will have noticed, the move to inquiry is the third stage of the research process — not first or second. You will undoubtedly have done a lot of work before you get to this point. Most researchers spend a great deal of time exploring the landscape simply to become expert enough to be able to ask a good question, one that is large enough for the size of the project and engaging enough to sustain their interest and energy. Storyteller and psychologist Reshad Field puts this nicely:

It had never occurred to me that the majority of so-called questions I had asked before were merely spontaneous pleadings. They
were not really based on experience and study. Now, after years of
training, I could, as it were, feel the question within me, but for
the life of me I could not get it into the right words . . . Finding the
exact question can be a subtle and difficult process. [126]

We place the formulation of the question here, after researchers have
had a chance to immerse themselves in the field of interest, because a
good research question is derived from an informed curiosity. It expresses fresh engagement with the field of interest, whether or not the field
of interest is a new one or, like some we have described, an old familiar
theme. In inquiry, researchers must enter the field anew and explore it
from its center to its edges. They encounter those who will become colleagues by virtue of their own work in this field. This is an act of collaborative scholarship. As such, it is often an initiation into the practice of
holding a question that has been left in the field — left particularly for the
researcher by others one might otherwise never know.

What is a question? What are its tone, its attitude, and its hope? This,
itself, is an important inquiry. Many students find that their relationship to research is dominated by a sense of responsibility or performance
anxiety — that there is something to show or prove. Right enough, one
must demonstrate one's credentials to engage in the research, so a feeling of pressure is natural. But pressure can be a problem when it pushes
a person to evade uncertainty because that, in turn, may prevent the researcher from formulating a real question — one that is not yet answered.
Researchers may instead phrase an idea or an assertion in terms of a question and think that is enough. It is not enough, because it hasn't got the
right measure of informed curiosity.

As a test, try to recall the feeling of curiosity. Bring to mind a time
when something in the world grabbed your attention and raised a sense
of question in you. This is a feeling that people register bodily, and it can
be contrasted to the feeling of being put on the spot to demonstrate what
you know already.

Once the attitude toward the topic has shifted, from one of interest
to one of inquiry, it is time to formulate a central research question. The

researcher can think of this as a refining process that involves a series of
steps or stages. It begins with the attitude of informed curiosity — a view
of the broad landscape which the researcher has already selected (or responded to) as one among many possibilities for study. It then narrows to
an aspect or piece of that landscape, which one can think of as identifying
the general question, issue, or problem; the *one* feature of the landscape
that attracts the researcher's attention. In thesis or dissertation work this
is often referred to as the research problem and is ultimately articulated
as the *statement of the problem*.

Consider again the role of pathologizing as it applies to the research
question. A natural tendency of the psyche is to present an urgent issue that desires attention as a problem. Similarly, one may think of the
research question as a source of urgency, embedded in the field of interest, yearning to be expressed as a problem. Polanyi describes this middle
phase of the refining process well. "All true scientific research starts with
hitting on a deep and promising problem, and this is half the discovery."[127] It is half the discovery, and it's an achievement to celebrate. But
it isn't yet a clear question that can guide the project. Researchers must
narrow the inquiry yet again until they are able to succinctly articulate
which particular question the work will address.

To demonstrate the process of formulating a central question, we'll
use Elizabeth's dissertation as an example. Elizabeth read and appreci-
ated the myth of Eros and Psyche as the only story in which Psyche is portrayed as an animated, autonomous figure instead of an arid concept. She
further refined her work by discovering that she didn't equally relish all
aspects of the myth. One key image fascinated her, Psyche's knife. In the
dissertation concept paper, Elizabeth tentatively put the central question
this way:

> What can we learn by "sticking to the image" of Psyche's knife and
> exploring why it has been overlooked and what it has to tell us?

Of course this is actually three questions built into one, but it was a
good starting point, particularly because it released a host of additional
questions. That proved to Elizabeth that there was enough richness and
complexity in the topic to sustain her interest over the long and some-

times lonely process of writing a dissertation. Elizabeth concluded her concept paper with this statement of intention:

> At this point in the process, I plan to sift through the questions that I have posed to find those with the most eros for me. Yes, it seems appropriate to allow archetypal Eros to be my guide into the material. However, I am going to keep Psyche's knife by my side, my conspirator in this journey who will, I hope, continue to visit my waking and sleeping dreams and help me to discriminate dross from gold.

It was evident in this phrasing that Elizabeth already knew which divinities she would propitiate. She also had a nascent sense that Psyche's knife symbolized the process of discrimination filtered through feeling or eros. When all was said and done, her first intuitive grasp of the project turned out to be clear and true. In the final draft of her dissertation, Elizabeth's statement of the problem ended up being very similar to the question she first formulated in the concept paper.

As we have noted, it is essential for psychological inquiry to begin in collaboration with the psyche and to remain collaborative. We have mentioned several of the forms this might take including ways to ritually invite Psyche into the work, personifying and dialoguing with the possible themes of the work, entering into an animated collegial relationship with the authors who have attended to these themes before us, and more. Since one of our primary goals is to underscore the need for such psychologically-based collaboration, we want to mention one fresh approach to collaborative inquiry — Participatory Action Research — that emphasizes collaboration from the earliest moments of the work. Participatory Action Research defers the articulation of the research question until the researcher has entered the community of interest, established a trusting relationship with indigenous members of the community, and involved them in the problem focus. In this way, the research question arises naturally from within the community of study itself.

Participatory Action Research seeks to address a host of political, economic, and social problems which characterize research that has failed to take the indigenous situation into sufficient account in the design and conduct of inquiry. It is a wonderful idea and we see it as another example of convergence between the needs for more psychologically informed modes of inquiry and recent developments in the field of social science. It is not vastly different from the ideas about collaboration already mentioned. Collaboration must begin and stay at the psychological level to truly be collaborative. Nevertheless, in Participatory Action Research, it is a matter of methodological importance that one refrains from imposing research questions from outside of a community of study. This would require a shift in the order of things as we have described them here.

A final word about formulating the central question of the work, borrowed from Immanuel Kant. In his *Critique of Pure Reason*, Kant said, "To know what questions may reasonably be asked is already a great and necessary proof of sagacity and insight."[128] We believe this is so because finding the question *tests* one's sagacity and insight and, in the process, brings psychological depth. Therefore wherever in the sequence this move occurs, it must occur for the inquiry to be psychological.

My topic seems to come to me not as a problem but as a matter of love and desire. I find it so fascinating that I just want to write about it. Where are the problem and the question in that kind of stance?

Not all writing is inquiry, not to mention psychological inquiry. Thank heaven for that! But assuming that your project wants to become a matter of psychological inquiry there are two possible solutions.

First, try to remember that love and desire are actually quite psychoactive and not always prone to happy endings. Explore your calling to this topic with a bit more complexity. What would happen if you started to feel differently about it? How does the topic itself resist inquiry and demand only love? What is the shadow side of this topic? Let's say that you have a long standing love for the work of a particular artist and just want to write a deep and appreciative commentary on it and what it means to you. You might need to read criticism of the artist that explores what makes the work brilliant and also reveals some problem worthy of note. For example, reading recent criticism of the music of Richard Strauss and its role in the Nazi cultural ethos might lead to a much richer appreciation of the artist than one might gain by leaving it out.

Second, try to hold your study accountable to some rather harsh critical questions; those being, "So what? What difference does this make to me or anyone? What gap might it fill?" A gap in the literature is, after all, a problem and it can usually generate a researchable question. If you do that and still end up feeling like the project is truly a matter of your own joy or entertainment why not just do it for that? Of course if you do, the project probably will not be suitable as academic research, a thesis or a dissertation.

The research question I'm drawn to has a lot of personal meaning for me and I'm not sure how much personal material ought to be in the final work.

This problem is actually a good sign. Remember that psychological inquiry is a matter of vocation or being called to the work. One usually experiences this at a very personal level, at least initially. The problem isn't whether the question has lots of personal meaning, but whether you have broadened your relationship to it through study and through the kinds of collaborative approaches already mentioned. If your relationship to the topic remains not only personal but deeply private, it may be that you have not really moved from topic to inquiry yet. You may be clinging to the topic the way we all do with our most cherished symptoms — as a matter of personal identity.

The important move here is not to try to diminish your personal relationship to the topic. Rather, through the development of informed curiosity, open up the field a bit to see *who else is there*. This is one way to engage in personifying. By collaborating with other persons inhabiting the field, you may gain the courage to ask true and researchable questions. It also increases the likelihood that while the work may hold deep personal meaning from beginning to end, it will, at the same time, be meaningful and valuable to others.

STAGE 4: EXTENDING THE RESEARCH

Most research projects will call for a proposal, which is designed to inform and persuade others of the merit of the work. With a thesis or dissertation one must work with an advisor or members of a committee to write a proposal. Once accepted, the research can begin. For a book proposal authors present a detailed outline and synopsis of the manuscript, along with information about themselves, the competition, and the audience, in order to find literary representation and secure a publishing contract. With a grant proposal, the researcher identifies the intention, scope, and feasibility of the study in the hope of gaining institutional support for the project. In all of these cases, the work is sufficiently formed, focused, and situated in a literary, scientific, or theoretical context that one can begin to imagine the project as a whole. The proposal encapsulates this whole and articulates the methods, moves, and course of study well enough to convince others that the work should go forward.

A proposal involves several key tasks. It should introduce the work by describing the area of interest and, depending on the circumstances, describe the nature of the researcher's calling to the work. It should provide enough of a review of pertinent literature to accomplish three important tasks: establishing a literary context for the work, deepening the conceptualization of the topic through contact with the writings of others, and leading to a horizon of the yet-to-be-known. It should articulate a clear statement of the problem and the specific research question or questions that the project will explore or discuss. It should propose a method for conducting the study and should provide a justification for that choice. Finally it should address some areas of concern that one should consider in this work, for example, strengths and weaknesses, human subjects considerations, cultural issues etc. Some hermeneutic approaches might also call for a proposed organization of the study laying out the lines of the hermeneutic inquiry one intends.

As one prepares the proposal it should take shape organically, meaning that it should grow in its own milieu. But for the purposes of writing clearly about each of its parts we will take them one at a time, beginning with a discussion of the literature review.

Reviewing the literature

The literature review is an extension and organization of the background reading. Recall in the discussion of background reading that we have encouraged you to read the literature in a consciously participatory way. Participatory reading can and should deepen now. The task is to enter into an animated relationship with the ideas and certainly with the authors. Allow yourself to become a host for imaginal conversations between readings from different contexts. In this way the literary field that surrounds your topic will gradually knit together, forming a lively matrix that can hold the fullness of the study.

Establishing a literary context for your work requires a substantial, if not comprehensive review of all the pertinent literature. This means that other scholars reading your work should not find it lacking in references to well known essays, articles, and books. The degree of breadth and depth this requires will vary greatly depending on how sharply the study is focused. Even if the work breaks new ground — and let's hope it does — you are entering into a landscape that already exists in some form. Others have walked at least some of the same territory. They may not have seen the things you see. They certainly have not seen it through your eyes. Nonetheless, it is the researcher's responsibility to know who has been there before and what they've had to say. Fundamentally, extending your research acknowledges the lineage of scholars that you are about to join. The hard work of scholarship pays respect to the masters that have gone before and the master that you yourself will someday become.

As you work the literature, you are also worked by it in many ways. One way in particular is that you begin to enter into a deeper conceptualization of the topic, transitioning from curious student to informed scholar. Along with this change, the topic and the question should mature as well. Their focus may become sharper or more diffuse depending on what needs to happen. It should feel a bit like looking through a microscope or telescope, once you know a bit more of what you are looking for, and adjusting the focal length until things come clear.

Finally, one's well informed relationship to the field makes it possible to assert not only what has been studied and written, but also what needs to be studied and written. What begins to take the place of personal attachment is a more collaborative sensibility in which the research question belongs to a field of which you are now a part. This is how a good literature review should function.

At this point, we want to call attention to two distinct modes of working the literature. Both are valid but they accomplish different things and should be taken up with intention and awareness. For purposes of instruction we can call these two modes *representation* and *interpretation*.

In representation, the researcher attempts a faithful restatement, in context, of what has been written. This requires withholding direct interpretation, comparison, and criticism for a time. Researchers do so to include the author's perspective as an autonomous participant in the study. An image of the representational mode of working the literature might be a large gathering of people seated at the community table, speaking on their own behalf. They can represent themselves better in their own words than if the researcher is seated alone at the table providing limited interpretive descriptions of what they have to say.

The other way of working the literature is the interpretive mode. Here, the researcher presents the literature in richly reconstructed context, emphasizing connections, comparisons, and critical reframing so that the individual contributions of each author are an important piece of a much larger point. At such a moment in the work you, the researcher, are the author by virtue of your interpretation of others' work. Of course one cannot really represent the literature without being somewhat interpretive, and that interpretation is a form of representation. Most researchers find themselves working in both modes, representational and interpretive. By differentiating them, we are encouraging you to use them responsibly and consciously, particularly when quoting the work of others.

The reason I have decided to work with this topic is that there is no substantial literature on it already. It is new and unexplored.

No ideas are so new or unique that they don't have parents, siblings, cousins, aunts and uncles. If you stay with the sense of things that lives in your question, your work will be lonely indeed. We refer again to the notion of a landscape. Some literary landscapes are like the city, overfull and growing with ideas and authors. Others might be more like the desert. But, even deserts have been written about.

It is important to remember that psychological inquiry is by definition collaborative work, and discovering your partners in this work is a joyful necessity. In our experience of advising students, the belief that there is nothing written about the topic reveals a particular kind of transference researchers have to the work — one that seems to require a symbiotic and very private orientation. It is akin to the feeling of having a problem that no one else can truly understand. Getting beyond such a limited view of the landscape is usually transformative and quite liberating.

I have this recurring nightmare that I will walk into the library or the bookstore and discover that someone has just published a book on my topic and done it better than I can.

This is an amazingly common fear, especially given that it is something that so rarely occurs. Earlier we said that there is no idea so new and different that nothing has been written on it. Also, no one can really write exactly what you are intending to write. Still, what you had hoped was going to be a completely new perspective or ground breaking idea may turn out to be quite well worked. That is the nature of the psyche: a reflection of humanity's collective curiosity and a repository of collective knowledge.

So what should researchers do when this nightmare appears to have come true? It will surely call for some shifts in how you hold the topic and in what the questions will become if the original ones have been answered. Putting it plainly, this situation will require reflection, probably consultation, and definitely imagination. The goal is to reframe the quandary and appreciate that you are not alone in the work — and then take up what remains to be explored.

Choosing a method

At the same time that shifts and refinements are taking place between researcher, topic, field, and question, the researcher gradually gains the ability to choose an approach or method. This happens for a few reasons. First, in reviewing the extant literature, researchers are exposed to methods used by others. With the benefit of hindsight, you can see what approaches have worked in response to what kinds of questions and in which topic areas. What have been the limitations and strengths of these projects? How does method shape the tone, style, and content of the final manuscript? All of your reading helps you to compare and evaluate different methods and choose one that suits you.

Second, it becomes apparent that some questions have particular affinity for certain methods. For example, if your question tends more toward a desire to understand the lived experience of a specific phenomenon — say the lived experience of being a graduate student above the age of 50 — it's very likely you would be inclined toward some qualitative method like phenomenology where interviews and other personal accounts provide the data for new insight. On the other hand you may find that your topic has settled upon some particular unexplored dialectic — two or more ideas that haven't yet been put into the same literary context and explored for their connections. For example, let's say you have had a long-standing interest in a particular form of artistic expression and you want to explore this for its connections to a particular theory of developmental psychology. You would want to place these two realms of literature and thought into a dialogue, and for that a hermeneutic approach would likely be best. Or, let's say you are interested in something a bit more dynamic or experimental, like the impact of certain pedagogical approaches on learning outcomes. For this you would most likely need to use some sort of quantitative method employing analysis of numerical data.

The point is that there is a determining relationship between the nature of the question and the best choice for approach and method. It simply would not make sense to try to answer a question about the lived experience of others, for example, without engaging others in the study. Nor would it make sense to try to answer a purely theoretical question with a great deal of complexity by using a reductive analysis of numerical data. Nor would it work well to inquire about the outcomes of a certain treatment strategy without gathering and analyzing some kind of experimental data. These statements may seem obvious, but our experience in teaching research tells us that students can easily become attached to a method in one frame of reference, but find themselves pursuing a topic in another. In such cases trying to put them together can produce awkward or disabling results. Better to let the method emerge organically as a product of refining the question through a strong review of the literature.

One way to see this issue from a psychological perspective is to imagine a kind of triangular relationship between you, the research question, and the method. Friends and lovers will recognize the complexity of the dynamic tensions in a triangle. Applied to research, imaging a triangular relationship offers some amazing insights. For example one might start out with a kind of erotic connection to a certain idea or theme — the topic. All is fine until one gets to the point of inviting a method into the mix. Let's say you choose a method that fits your character, but isn't a particularly good fit for the topic and question. As the method and the topic start to get together they will change each other to fit. It is not long before the topic and the researcher are wondering about each other. In a case like that, if the commitment to method is too rigid, the topic and the method may run off together leaving you, the researcher, to do all the work and have none of the joy. You can play with this triangle in a multitude of ways yourself, imagining different scenarios. They are all possible. But if you begin to work with this triangular dynamic, seeing it as a psychological reality with its own life force, you will be in a better position to foster a growing and balanced relationship between yourself, your topic, and your method.

In Chapter 2, the discussion on the history of qualitative methods revealed that inquiry into complex phenomena often requires an innova-tive approach to method. If the method does not serve the inquiry, it is the method that must change. Although an established and well articu-lated method often will serve — there are many to choose from after all — you may find that blending or revising established methods assists the inquiry. As far as we know none of the methods that are canonized in texts have been delivered by divine intervention. They are all inventions, most of them quite recent.

Invented or not, method plays an important role in framing, guid-ing, and containing research. It plays an equally important role in under-standing, evaluating, and critiquing research. In fact, following a method faithfully imparts its own ritual value. Scholar and Professor Rosemarie Anderson, author of an intriguing new method of qualitative research she named Intuitive Inquiry, has something to say on this topic.[129] Intuitive Inquiry is a blend of parts of other methods including heuristics, herme-neutics, phenomenology, and collaborative strategies that derive from feminist approaches. As the author of the method, Anderson knows first hand the give and take reasoning behind its invention. Nonetheless she holds herself accountable to its prescribed processes. Anderson makes the point that there is great value in submitting to a coherent method, whatever it might be. It becomes a ritual of submission to the work and can ultimately create a more collaborative environment. Putting the project under the control of a method creates a map of sorts, which others can follow to understand what has been done. It also removes the researcher from the central place. The method, not the ego of the researcher, works the topic and the data. Anderson's insight is valuable for many reasons. Among others, it illuminates our claim that although methodological innovation and flexibility are necessary to keep the work vitally linked to a world in flux, methodological rigor is also necessary to keep the work on task and comprehensible.

Even if your aim is to operate without method, it will take a method to do so, because it has become clear that method is present in the most elemental processes of research. From reading to conceptualizing and on through to writing researchers deal with implicit forms and methods built into language itself.

In preparing a proposal researchers must either choose an existing method or mix up a new one. The method section of the proposal can vary from being a few pages in length to an entire chapter. What it covers is more important than how long it is. First, the method section should contain reiterations of the problem statement and the research question, and a brief analysis of the implicit connections between the framing of the question and the possible methods. In other words, how does this type of question lend itself to particular approaches or methods as previously described? Second, it should describe other research on the topic that uses an approach or method different from the one you are proposing. By doing a comparative analysis of the methods, you distinguish your study from others and clarify your contribution to the field. Third, the method section should explore the philosophical background for the method you are choosing and make a clear case for why it is the best approach for your project. This should include speculation about the strengths and weaknesses of using this approach for this type of study.

It is becoming increasingly common for researchers to use parts or moves from different methods to invent a new method that fits this particular study better than anything off the rack. In these cases the method section will also need to address the logic of the mix. How was it conceived and how is it necessarily different from the methods from which it is derived? Methodological innovation actually calls for more methodological literacy and rigor than might be required if researchers were to simply choose a standardized, accepted method. Such innovation may be necessary in order to respond to the complex and shifting needs of psychological inquiry.

I have been reading a lot on methodology and find myself getting more confused and even frustrated. None of the methods I have studied really seem to address the themes and the phenomena that I am focusing on.

Psychological inquiry requires a very thoughtful, reflective, and yet rigorous relationship to the task of choosing a method. This task begins with a substantial degree of literacy in methodology but it cannot end there. Researchers should engage the question of method in a psychological way. For example one student, whose topic involved a complex issue related to personality and character, had spent many hours reading the literature and forming some research questions but had been unable to choose a method. Hermeneutics would allow him to work the literature in ways he was truly enjoying whereas phenomenology would provide a more experiential exploration of the topic. This student had even gone to the trouble of writing up two method sections to decide which approach would be best. Then one night he had a dream that he was sitting at a large table with many of the authors he had been reading, telling them his dreams. The authors were applauding him, recognizing the wisdom of the dreams as they related to his topic.

After reflecting on his dream about dreams, the student discovered a way to combine theoretical hermeneutic work with lived experience. He included several of his own dreams as additional texts, submitting them to a structured analysis the way one works interview material in a phenomenological study. Then he integrated the dream material into the hermeneutic process of reviewing the literature. The blend worked quite well. In this case, it is apparent that the field of interest lives not only in the books on library shelves. In psychological inquiry the field is psychoactive and lives in the spaces one makes for it. From there, topic and method can speak even in dreams if one is willing to pay attention.

Writing the proposal

The structure of the written proposal is often governed by those for whom it is written. We discussed what must be included in a typical proposal for a thesis or dissertation at the beginning of this section. Beyond structure and form let's examine how the proposal functions at a psychological level by considering it from the standpoint of its images.

First, the proposal is anchored by what has been done already, but it looks forward to what is yet to be done. As such, a proposal evokes the image of a threshold, which is oriented toward a horizon. In most cases this orientation is mirrored by the fact that a proposal is written substantially in the future tense. Researchers are proposing what they will be doing once the proposal is approved. In addition, a proposal is like a gathering of colleagues in that it introduces the assembled allies of the study — those authors whose work forms the basis of, and the calling for, this study. It sets a course that the researcher is committed to complete, at least at the outset. Changes can occur down the line, as the work requires it, but at the point of submitting the proposal there is a felt sense of commitment to the work as proposed. Finally, the proposal attests to the researcher's readiness for the work and the desire to make a contribution to the field. In all this one might hold the image of a person standing on a prominent threshold surrounded by those who support the work or have an interest in it. This person pauses there to be seen and acknowledged before entering into service and embarking on a quest. The proposal is a significant marker in the work. It represents the culmination of a great deal of thought and effort and the beginning of a new set of ideas, concerns, and relationships.

STAGE 5: COMPLETING THE WORK

The final phase in a research project is the completion of the work committed to in the proposal. Very likely this phase will be the largest in volume and it may take the longest time. In our experience, however, researchers have already done so much solid preparatory work that completing the project is usually less stressful than preparing the proposal, and often more fun. This phase will include the activities of gathering and analyzing the data, writing up the research results or findings, and preparing the final, fully complete manuscript. Because there are so many different methods and modes researchers can follow at this point, each of which are guided by the proposal, we will not focus here on particular processes. Instead we will consider the ways that one needs to move to hold the work solidly in the realm of psychological inquiry.

Before beginning the processes of completing the work it is a good idea for the researcher to undertake a comprehensive review of the entire proposal. The timing of this review may seem a bit odd, since it follows the commitment to the work one has so carefully and comprehensively articulated. But in most cases there is a period of time between submitting a proposal and its approval. The approval process alone invites a critical review, whether by colleagues, committee members, or the researcher. As you enter the field with a more elaborate map and a more refined sense of your destination or goal, it simply makes sense to look again. Re-examine the problem statement and the questions. Reconsider the literary field that you have circumscribed. Definitely re-examine the method. Do all this with an eye and an ear toward keeping the work alive and engaged. In all likelihood, this review will reaffirm the rightness of the proposal. But if you are open to it, it may also be the occasion of some important reconsiderations and realignments that will help you reach your goals. There are some methods, Grounded Theory Methodology[130] for example, that formally include this kind of review so that the themes, processes, and theory-making are continually subject to adjustment. But in most approaches this kind of course correction is much more difficult and less available once you have worked the data and come to the final phase of writing.

My project is a theoretical study using a hermeneutic approach. I have lots of good material and I have done a good job developing theory but I can't help feeling I should do some interviews to get other people's perspectives into the work.

Including the voices of other humans in the process through interviewing provides an interactive collaborative feel to research. But your work with the literature also has been an opportunity to consider a variety of perspectives. Perhaps you need to do a critical review of your work

with the literature and see if there are ways that you have not fully repre-
sented, or perhaps over-interpreted, the perspectives of others. If, on the
other hand, the topic needs more engaged and interactive input, and you
are still able to change your method, you might need to do so. If it is too
late to change it, consider incorporating a *resonance panel* in your research,
a move that is part of Rosemarie Anderson's Intuitive Inquiry.[131] The
resonance panel is group of well-informed participants who review your
findings with you and give you feedback, which you then integrate into
the work. Working with a resonance panel is one of several possible approaches that would provide the kind of live collaboration you long for at
this late date. .

    There may also be some ways that you are reacting to your own voice
in the work and that could fall under the heading of transference. You
might try reading some pertinent passages using the approach developed
by Romanyshyn and Goodchild discussed earlier in Chapter 4. This may
lead to a need for an altogether different correction than simply adding
some interviews.

Gathering and analyzing the data

The raw material of research is the data. When researchers set up the
project it will include a determination as to the type of data they will
gather, where it will come from, and how they will work it. Most articulated methods include a strong focus on these processes to ensure they
are rational, effective, and ethical. Consequently, this stage of the research
process is closely scrutinized in all critical evaluations of the final work.
Has the project succeeded in gathering the right kind of data from the
right sources to adequately address the concerns and answer the questions it has posed? Has the data been analyzed in a rational, systematic,
and thorough way so that the findings make sense given the data? If human subjects were involved, have they been treated ethically and shielded
from unnecessary harm and exposure? These are the typical questions
used to evaluate research projects. In psychological inquiry one needs to
go further.

    By now it should be very clear that psychological inquiry requires
researchers to make every effort to keep the data alive — to keep the

work from killing it. Unfortunately scholarly and scientific inquiries have often emphasized descriptive and taxonomic approaches to data so that the differences between a living being and a cadaver aren't much of an issue. This is not sufficient where the psyche is concerned.

In addressing the psyche one needs to keep things in movement. A nice image to represent this is the butterfly. (In art and literature the butterfly is a common symbol for the psyche, with its connections to metamorphosis and transformation.) One can study the butterfly in a variety of ways. In a taxonomic descriptive approach, one of the primary tools is the *kill jar:* a jar into which the researcher places the creature, killing it without damaging its form, so that he can examine it closely. Eventually, the researcher will pin the butterfly to a board so he can look at it whenever he wishes. Using the kill jar is certainly easier than chasing butterflies across a field in the hopes of catching a glimpse of the creature. But it does miss some things, doesn't it? It will miss the butterfly's flight, its social life, and its responses to the environment. Moreover, it will miss the processes of transformation that are essential to understanding the nature of the butterfly. Contrast the use of the kill jar with placing yourself in the habitat of the butterfly and taking the time to enter its world. Consider what it would be like to devote yourself to the study of the living creature, which includes the dark sleepy underworld of the butterfly's life as pupae. It is quite a profound difference. In psychological inquiry, researchers need to avoid capturing data in kill jars. The study should be designed so that the aliveness of the data is preserved. One can do this by holding the data, as much as possible, within its context. Allow it to reverberate there, even if the risk is some degree of confusion or added complexity.

For example, in working with dream images, rather than simply naming the image, or worse, assigning it a reductive analytical interpretation, you would try to represent the image more in the context of the dream and allow it to continue moving. Upon reflection, many of the moves described here — collaboration, dialogue, moves of language, working the transference — carry some emphasis on this task of keeping the data alive. It is tricky but it's doable. Once you begin to think and write this way, you will find that a living butterfly is much more informative than a dead one — much more available to guide the transformations you hope for.

In choosing the methods and processes of research, particularly in regard to gathering and analyzing data, psychological inquiry requires some moments in the wild. This is the habitat of the protean psyche, where living things describe each other through movement.

Writing and editing the manuscript

Researchers who complete the proposal have, of course, already been engaged in the task of writing part of the manuscript. Nonetheless, as you embark on writing the remaining chapters, there often is a new sense of excitement, anticipation, and perhaps anxiety that accompanies this step. It is the beginning of the rest of the task, which will only end when you have a complete manuscript in your hands. At this point it may be worthwhile to consider an apparently simple-minded question: "What is writing, anyway?"

In our courses and seminars, we make a distinction between writing and rewriting. Writing is what happens when someone faces the blank page, paper or electronic, and composes sentences, paragraphs, and ultimately whole sections of text. Writing is fresh: the first gleanings from the researcher's mind and soul. Writing expresses the thoughts and ideas that have swirled about during months of background reading and preparatory research, conversations with colleagues and friends, counsel from mentors and experts in the field. Writing is essential to maintain what was described earlier in the chapter as an ecology of creativity. If one imagines research as taking in and mulling over the ideas of others, then writing is releasing or expressing the researcher's thoughts and observations that have been nourished and seasoned by the research. Too much research without enough writing tends to stifle the creative process of producing a completed manuscript. Writing helps researchers see the evolution of their understanding of the topic, which includes exposing areas in which they have achieved some mastery and also areas that are confusing, obscure, or simply calling for more attention. As one of our students said, people write to learn as much as they learn to write.

If writing is capturing fresh ideas on the blank page, rewriting, or editing, is working over those ideas. One rewrites for many reasons. Some are:

to enrich the prose by adding subtlety and nuance; to extend the prose by adding other perspectives, including complementary or dissenting ideas; to deepen the prose by faithful consideration of what has not been said or considered. This kind of editing is generative because it encourages the flow of ideas. To imagine generative rewriting, think of an intricate and extensive river system arising from a source deep in the mountains. Small rivulets join creeks, which join larger tributaries that ultimately feed the main channel of water flowing to the sea. Rewriting that serves the work is a combination of following the flow to see where it leads and shaping the material to keep the flow going. Another metaphor is dream analysis. Does the attention you give to the page foster deeper, richer, and more plentiful associations? Does your editing produce more meanings and new insights? Or does it wind in on itself tighter and tighter, reducing meaning and restricting the flow of your prose? If the latter case is true, you may be doing obsessive rewriting, not generative rewriting.

Obsessive rewriting does not serve the creative process. It tends to be exacting, overly critical, and reductive — all of which stop the flow of ideas from the author to the page. It may kill an idea that you've already put into words and also close the door to new ideas that are waiting for your attention. Author Victoria Nelson, in her excellent book *On Writer's Block*, alludes to this. She calls obsessive rewriting "nonwriting":

> Forced writing often leads to another kind of nonwriting — namely, the compulsion to rework projects to death . . . Here I refer to a tendency to kill a living work by repeated surgery, amputations, transplants, and the like under the merciless glare of your analytical (not creative) attention. [132]

Nelson points out a key difference between generative and obsessive rewriting, which is the quality of attention one brings to the task. The glare of the obsessive editor is merciless. The gaze of the creative editor is characterized by the same qualities that make psychological inquiry so meaningful: curiosity, playfulness, and wonder.

As you work on each chapter, you will sometimes be engaged in writing and sometimes in rewriting. One student begins each writing day by reading what she wrote in the preceding session. Sometimes she makes minor revisions to a section; sometimes the revisions are more extensive; sometimes there are none at all. In all cases, the rereading refreshes her orientation to the topic before she faces the blank page once again. The point is, in actual practice rewriting is often difficult to separate entirely from writing. Nor is there any reason to make a sharp distinction. We recommend that you pay attention to the kind of rewriting you are doing and ask yourself whether or not it serves the work.

When you finish writing an entire chapter, it is a good idea to put it aside for a short while, perhaps a week or two, or even a month, before beginning the task of editing the chapter as a whole. Professional writers who have some breathing room in their schedules know such a period of rest can make a big difference in the quality of their editing. The idea is to approach a completed chapter with fresh eyes. Not only does this help you catch typos and other minor errors in the manuscript, it can also alert you to problems in organization, flow, and clarity. In addition, such a review can take you more deeply into the transferential aspects of the work as was discussed in Chapter 4. Read the chapter silently, and note where there is any kind of question or confusion. Where are you stopped? What might this mean? Read the chapter aloud and listen for subtle nuances in writing tone, style, and rhythm. Is your voice consistent? Does it sound the way you want it to? If there are places in the chapter where the voice shifts, stop and pay attention. Give yourself time to reflect on the possible meanings of the shift and decide what to do about it.

One student read her work in these ways and found that her sentences tended to be long, complicated and quite formal when she was discussing current research in her subject area. Upon reflection, she thought she needed to sound like a scholar and had unconsciously adopted a stiff tone that created distance between the topic and her self. Her writing style at other moments in the chapter, especially when she described her personal associations to the research question, was very different; more engaged, vivid, and intimate. There is nothing wrong with using different voices if they serve the work. We simply urge you to become aware of them.

If you are doing a thesis or dissertation it is essential to work closely with your committee as you complete the project. Remember they are your allies. This doesn't mean, however, committee members will simply support you. Often the most worthwhile allies are individuals who are not afraid of opposing you. This loyal opposition may take the form of criticism, suggestions for improvement, or observations about an overlooked aspect of the topic. This is a moment to remember the move of collaboration defined previously: openness to difference. Though you are the sole author of the work, the members of your committee are, or should be, full collaborators in its production. To the best of your ability, take each comment and suggestion as an opportunity to deepen the work and your relationship to it. Remember that each of us operates within a perspective at all times. Your committee members operate from their perspective, and if you can allow it, they will help you turn the work to expose its many facets in the same way a jeweler appreciates a gemstone.

Releasing the work

The final preparation of the complete manuscript is an opportunity to reflect on the project as a whole. Some surprising insights often occur at this stage. It may even be the first time that you fully appreciate what you have created and what role it has played in your own transformation. Taking the time to read the work as a whole, perhaps over the course of a weekend or as part of a retreat, can be a very moving experience. It is an opportunity for the gestalt of the creation to make itself known. It also is an opportunity to reflect on Jung's point that it is not the author that creates the work, but the work that creates the author, as he puts it so beautifully in this quote:

> It makes no difference whether the artist knows that his work is generated, grows, and matures within him, or whether he imagines that it is his own invention. In reality it grows out of him as a child its mother. The creative process has a feminine quality, and the creative work arises from unconscious depths — we might truly say from the Mothers. Whenever the creative force predominates, life is ruled and shaped by the unconscious rather than the conscious will . . . The progress of the work becomes the poet's fate and determines his psychology.[133]

The metaphor of childbirth that Jung uses has another meaning for this stage of the process. It is imperative to release the work to the world in the same way that gestation is completed by birth. This moment can be both exhilarating and terrifying. Often, questions of adequacy arise. Is the work enough? Have I done well? Is it truly complete? This is where one returns to one of the more perplexing aspects of psychological inquiry. Yes, the work is complete, but it is not finished. In psychological inquiry, the final manuscript is a living being; a psychic entity in its own right. In the best of all outcomes, it becomes one of the many voices taking its rightful place in an ongoing dialogue on your topic that others, also engaged in inquiry, will respond to. If your work has been a true vocation — and we hope this is the case — your relationship to it will continue to grow and evolve, beckoning you to other creative thresholds.

6

HONORING THE SPIRIT OF PLAY

As we draw this book to a close, we want to return to an image and an idea mentioned in the opening paragraph. Our guiding spirit in this endeavor has been the archetypal child who continues asking questions for the sheer delight of exploration and discovery. We have been speaking on behalf of play in every chapter and our premise invites appreciative attention to a child's natural vivacity. The art of inquiry is grounded in a fully reciprocal and participatory relationship with the world; a relationship characterized by openness, enthusiasm, curiosity, and wonder. In this final chapter, we honor the spirit of the archetypal child and meditate on the value of play.

By saying right up front that a depth psychological perspective is one way to approach inquiry, we are urging you, our reader, to play with it. What does this perspective reveal? How does it help re-imagine one's relationship to the work? How do the insights of depth psychology enliven other traditions of inquiry? In Chapter 2 we have told a story about the origins of qualitative research, knowing full well that another storyteller would very likely tell it differently. That doesn't make our story right and the others wrong. This is not intended as a rejection of other narratives. If you, the reader, allow curiosity to be your guide, each telling can enhance your knowledge and understanding of the richness of qualitative research. In Chapter 3 we offer a laundry list of philosophical commitments, which we fervently hope is not the last word on the subject. We want you to entertain the ideas and let them entertain you. Use them as building blocks to construct your own understanding of the psyche and maybe add a few of your own. We end Chapter 3 with a discussion of the dialectical nature of the psyche, attesting to the dynamic relationship between ideas that are continually in play with one another. Inquiry guided by the psyche must be equally dynamic, engaged, and playful. In Chapters 4 and 5, we advocate move over method in order to help you adopt the natural fluidity of research that is guided by the psyche. Such research is surprisingly dynamic, particularly when it is released from the rigidity of slavish adherence to formal method. We may say that the lived experience of inquiry is characterized by invention more than intention no matter how much rigorous planning and control you bring to the process. Ideas and words love to play, so naturally there are unexpected turns, starts, and stops as you gather and arrange ideas and let them flow onto the printed page.

As advocates of psychological inquiry, it isn't very surprising that our guiding spirit is the archetypal child. This image has held a place of considerable influence in depth psychology for the last century. In Freud's work, the child appears primarily as a symbol of the past. Freud searched for the etiology of the neuroses in childhood, and discovered that the memories his adult patients repressed were the source of their illness. Moreover, the very structure of the adult psyche and the core of its conscious identity, including the ego and the superego, were shaped by the child's earliest experiences. Freud dwelled on the child in another context more closely related to the art of inquiry. In his essay "Creative Writers and Daydreaming," he theorized that creativity shares an important attribute with childhood play; both require intense engagement and an investment of large amounts of emotion because the child "takes his play very seriously." [134] For the child, play is not trivial or frivolous. Spontaneous, daring, dynamic, imaginative, and surprising yes. But trivial? No. Paradoxically, it is the serious nature of play that hints at its generative power and suggests why play and creativity are so closely related to one another.

In Jung's writings, the archetypal child is the divine child who reminds people that "life is a flux, a flowing into the future, not a stoppage or a backwash." The divine child prefigures "the synthesis of conscious and unconscious elements of the personality," symbolizing the self that will grow, over time, into wholeness. [135] For this reason, the divine child motif also symbolizes the process of individuation, which is the telos of psychological life. As we discussed in Chapter 3, this telos is not meant to be taken literally, as Jung made plain: "Psychic wholeness," he said, "will never be attained empirically" because the conscious mind is "too narrow and too one-sided to comprehend the full inventory of the psyche."[136] The value of psychic wholeness as a telos is its mythic sensibility, which always alludes to places one has yet to visit, ideas one cannot quite articulate, and insights one has not received. The idea of a telos suggests the distance between reach and grasp and the desire that arcs like a flow of electrical current between them. This is where the theme of play arises again, and why the divine child is such a powerful image of the future. People individuate by moving toward what presents itself as *other* in their lives in much the same way children, guided only by their eagerness to explore what they have never encountered, discover their delight in the things of the world. This kind of play is a commitment of time as well as emotion, intellect, sensation, and imagination.

It is thus easy to imagine how the spirit of the archetypal child that infuses creative work, and guides psychological inquiry, spills over into other areas of life. This is the best possible outcome because inquiry is more than asking questions. It is an active, reciprocal relationship with the world that can last through the completion of a creative project or endure for a lifetime. Above all, it demands a person's wholehearted participation at the levels of body, mind and soul. Sometimes, this participation requires the active *yang* posture of seeking knowledge, understanding, or insight. At others, it requires a receptive *yin* posture that provokes the anxiety of not doing enough, as though accomplishment is the only measure of life well lived. But accomplishment is not the *sine qua non* of the good life and the urge to solve problems or regulate chaos is not the ego's sole task. When psychological inquiry becomes a way of life, attention to the soul's needs and desires takes precedence. The conscious ego serves the soul by adopting the subtle, paradoxical consciousness that Marie-Louise von Franz speaks of in which one develops an ear for complexity, an eye for obscurity, and a feel for fluidity. Then the psyche becomes real. Then one's own soul and the soul of the world become expressive others that compel attention and draw the person into the labyrinths of a rich and meaning-filled life.

THE REALITY OF THE PSYCHE

Over the course of this book we have attempted to show what it means to accept the reality of the psyche when conducting research. We have even alluded to what it means when living a life. In Chapter 1, we discussed Socrates, a pivotal figure whose call to think for oneself has become a defining principle of what it means to be a person. For Socrates, the central reality of human life was the psyche. Though depth psychology as a formal discipline began about 2400 years later, it reinvigorated the classical tradition of inquiry on behalf of the soul, and Socrates' own story still provides some of the first and best clues about living a psychological life. Psychological life is practicing what Socrates called piety and what we have described as reverence towards all living things, including the living psyche in its many forms. Psychological life is devoted to continual inquiry, relishing the *pursuit* of wisdom more than the *possession* of it. It is the willingness to learn from everyone and everything by reflecting on others' ideas without defensiveness. It is the ability to be deeply moved by what one sees, hears, and feels, accepting the full impact of living in complex emotional bodies. It is tolerating periods of personal doubt and confusion created by meaningful engagement with other perspectives. It is looking past the surface of things to their interior depths and their transcendent source. Finally, it is holding ideas, images, and beliefs lightly so that one can witness and learn from their inherent playfulness.

In other words, once one declares that the psyche is real, one grows increasingly aware of the actual complexity and fluidity of lived experience. Jung alluded to developing such awareness when he spoke about the "richness of mind" necessary to psychological life.

> Richness of mind consists in mental receptivity, not in the accumulation of possessions. What comes to us from outside, and, for that matter, everything that rises up from within, can only be made our own if we are capable of an inner amplitude equal to that of the incoming content. [137]

This statement directly opposes the idea that riches are the cumulative result of hoarding. Rather, richness has everything to do with a concept that seems particularly at odds with contemporary Western values: emptying, or emptiness. Psychological life is not a matter of stuffing oneself full of experiences or ideas or images and holding tightly to the known. It is not a matter of constructing a towering ego from which one deigns to condescend to the world — and beat a hasty retreat to the top of that tower should the world insinuate itself into one's certainties. Richness of mind develops by opening oneself to a variety of "content" (to use Jung's surprisingly modern word) and welcoming all of it. As discussed in Chapter 4, hospitality is paramount. It is similar to a child's invitation to "c'mon out and play." The result is mutual enrichment that expands the mind and soul and creates the inner amplitude, or capacity, that makes ongoing play possible.

The growth of inner amplitude that Jung spoke of mirrors the way of the cosmos. In fact, there is one monumental discovery about the universe that is nearly impossible to grasp. Since its birth, the universe has been growing larger, but not from a central point. It is both expanding and polycentric, which means it has many centers, each of which is growing alongside every other. The evolution of the universe from its earliest beginnings until now exemplifies the way of all nature. To evolve is to expand without sacrificing complexity or multiplicity. While this insight has received the attention it warrants as a discovery about the physical universe, and Jung appears to have had an intuition about it as a psychological idea, it has yet to fully be explored.

One author who suggests the psychological implications of this discovery is cosmologist Brian Swimme, who speaks about the huge, numinous powers filling the universe. It is simply not human, he declares, to live a life that is sealed off from all conscious contact with these powers. They are immanent in every part of creation and within every cell.[138] And humans are such stuff as the universe is made of. If so, isn't the cosmos suggesting that expansion and multiplicity is also human nature? It is. Living a small, narrow-minded and rigid life is an *opus contra naturam*. People are not here to construct impermeable boundaries around themselves, cultivating control in order to remain aloof from the world. Participating in the expansion of the universe asks people to live as vastly as they possibly can by seeking unfathomable depths of soul, both the personal soul and the soul of the world. This participation challenges people to maintain the shape of their unique character while at the same time permitting the playful, spontaneous, and fluid give-and-take necessary to grow into their fullest form. Jung called this individuation. It is the essence of psychological life.

Most people don't choose to live as vastly as they can. For many, it's frightening and uncomfortable because it means exposing oneself to "the undefined and indefineable," which Jung described as the "spiritual adventure of our time." [139] Instead of pushing past the walls of self-created prisons people are inclined to occupy one small corner of a habitual existence and defend it with territorial ferocity. By accepting small, constricted lives they relinquish their birthright as creatures of the expanding cosmos.

What has happened in history that calls humanity to remember something so obvious? Rather than being separate, people are thoroughly embedded in and interconnected with their giant cosmic home. Scores of books have been written in answer to this question, among them Richard Tarnas's masterful account of the long 2500-year arc of western consciousness, *The Passion of the Western Mind,* and Charlene Spretnak's *States of Grace.* They are beautiful and eloquent testimonials to modernity's insane bargain. Humanity has asserted control of the world through the subjugation of the other and, in exchange, has developed a profound sense of alienation. Homelessness, though uncomfortable, has become acceptable. This homelessness is occasionally glorified as freedom as though one could discard attachments to people, places and professions as easily as one might discard consumables that have served their purpose and are valuable no more. Yet how impoverished life becomes without them! Hobbes's famous description of human life as "solitary, poor, nasty, brutish and short" expresses this impoverishment in five pithy adjectives. Hobbes, steeped in the scientific materialism of his age, viewed the natural world as dead, inert material, valuable only as the stuff of clever experiments designed to further human progress. This view prevailed in eighteenth-century Europe and continues to shape the values of modern technological society. According to this belief, interrelationship with *Gaia,* a living earth that includes both human and more-than-human inhabit-

ants, is silly, childish, and repugnant. Believing one is a vital, interconnected part of the immensity of the cosmos is even sillier.

Living a psychological life opposes the prevailing cultural attitude.
Humanity is measured by attentive, compassionate, and conscious participation with Gaia. Psychological life is redolent with meaning and depth.
One is invited to become more aware of how the smallest action and
most subtle beliefs have consequences for everyone and everything one
encounters. One sees self and other as deeply rooted in the *anima mundi*,
the soul of the world; Psyche herself. Perhaps more important, psychological life invites people to perceive the ways in which Psyche is rooted
in them. To do so, one must follow her playful, inquisitive ways and live
the questions that reflect the natural activities of the soul. "Who's here?"
honors the psyche's complexity and fluidity and recognizes all the persons who populate it. "What's wrong?" honors Psyche's mode of speaking
in symptoms, or what is painful to perceive or feel or address. "What
does it mean?" honors the psyche's penchant for poetic, suggestive, and
multi-layered renderings of literal things so that their symbolic richness
becomes apparent.

LIVING IN AN ANIMATED WORLD

If it was an easy matter to recall seeing the world with a child's sense of
wonder, it would not be necessary to say much on behalf of the animated
world. The animated world would simply be a fact of existence, and play
would come far more easily. The sad fact is that few adult activities are
as animated, spontaneous, and engaged as child's play. Adult imagination
is yoked to problem solving or planning, not simple enjoyment. Unlike
children, modern adults tend to treat the things of the world as inert objects rather than expressive subjects. It seems that people notice the *anima
mundi* only when they are moving at a slow, thoughtful pace. Perhaps this
is why the French philosopher Gaston Bachelard pointed out that reverie "is under the sign of anima." [140] Reverie invites one into a relationship with the soul of the world, deeply attuned to everything that shows
up. Time slows down, becoming magnificent and stately. Language and
thought become less self-centered and more world noticing, reverent,

and celebratory. The recognition that soul is in the world may awaken people, Hillman remarks, "from the psychotherapeutic trance in which we pay a hundred dollars for an hour of subjectivism and no more than $19.95 for a beach chair in whose cold metallic arms and plastic lap reflection actually takes place, day after day." [141]

Contemporary culture does not explicitly denounce reverie or play, but they were condemned nonetheless as two distinct cultural streams flowed together: the Scientific Revolution and the Protestant Reformation. Early in the seventeenth century, "grasping the order of the cosmos through contemplation came to be seen as vain and misguided, a presumptuous attempt to escape the hard work of detailed discovery." Knowledge arrived at through imagination or contemplation was considered "specious; for technological gain is the criterion of genuine knowledge." [142] Use and useful work became the standard of judgment. Idleness, which included both play and reverie, was of the devil. As creatures of a creator God, it was the duty of all to use the gifts He gave and to work for the good of His (human) creation. But, people were to do so without loving their work or things of the world. Such worldliness would divert love from its proper object, a transcendent God. Puritan preachers constantly repeated these two messages: idleness was the very devil and so was love of the world. In a sermon given by Richard Sibbes in 1637, he expressed this position clearly:

> Where the world hath got possession in the heart, it makes us false to God, and false to man, it makes us unfaithfull in our callings, and false to Religion it selfe. Labour therefore to have the world in its owne place, under thy feet. Labour to know the world that thou maiest detest it. [143]

Puritan teachings are certainly less common now, and only a few Christian preachers in this day and age might urge their flock to detest the world. Do people still seek ways to dominate matter rather than cherish it? Sadly, the answer is yes.

Cultural antipathy to a vital and intimate relationship with a sacred world has been described by the historian and sociologist Charles Taylor as the "disengaged, instrumental stance." *Instrumentalizing* is rational rather than sensual, controlling rather than receptive, and frigid rather than fluid. It is oriented towards use and usefulness. Activities such as play and reverie, which produce no visible results or goods, are anathema. As Taylor explains, the instrumental stance allows humanity "to experiment and obtain valid scientific results" in addition to granting people "rational control over themselves and the world." For the Puritans, it is the "spiritually essential step.[144]

The instrumental stance leaves little room for mystery and even less for grace. Instead, people are confident that the created order is entirely scrutable and their task is to analyze it down to the last detail. They are not supposed to love the world with a childlike sense of delight or even stand in awe of its grandeur. Instead people are expected to dominate the world. If a person consistently and exclusively adopts the instrumental stance toward the world, the world presents itself as a non-stop assortment of problems or challenges to be solved and tasks to be accomplished. While this approach develops a person's valuable strategic and analytical abilities, it tends to discourage more receptive feeling abilities and the willingness to be whimsical, adventurous, or spontaneous. The problem is that Western culture urges the adoption of the instrumental stance so consistently and subtly that it happens unconsciously, leaving people unaware of what has been lost in the process.

Consider, for example, one of C.G. Jung's lesser-known and more disturbing observations: *Professionalism condemns us to be competent.* Why disturbing? People expect to dominate every situation or, failing that, to act *as if* they have everything under control. American culture prizes control in every arena whether or not it is ostensibly professional. This expectation of competence is so prevalent that it places the harsh demands of competitive success even on leisure activities. Leisure is not idle. Leisure is merely another form of activity, and a particularly intense activity at that. One must not merely play for the sheer fun of trying something new, heedless of the outcome. The ubiquitous Nike advertising campaign of the last decade, for example, may use the words "Just Do It," but the images that accompany those words convey an entirely different sensibility. Do it "right," and look "right" doing it. In American business and American culture, second place is the first loser.

The most invidious form that this expectation of competence takes is in the conduct of life itself. People must know exactly whom they are, what they are doing, and where they are going. Stasis is inexcusable or pathological; so is spontaneity and experimentation unless, of course, they lead to success. Even the realization that this treadmill existence is self imposed is not always enough to permit stopping. The idea of not doing is nearly inconceivable. For instance, a friend decided last year that her New Year's resolution was to accomplish nothing. After the laughter died down — can anyone really resolve to accomplish nothing? — there was a long, lingering silence. In those moments, each of us wondered what our lives would be like if we just *lived* them instead of *did* them. Americans are so steeped in the Puritan work ethic that it was virtually inconceivable.

FROM DESCARTES'S ERROR TO THE BODYMIND

People are not talking heads, or bodies controlled by an appendage called the brain that dictates every move through life. Rather, they are bodymind, an intricate blend of invisible thought and tangible matter. As discussed in Chapter 3, the first depth psychologists recognized the body-mind connection and named this extended organism the psyche. Today, leading neuroscientists have recently affirmed what Freud and Jung claimed a century ago, agreeing that mind is not located in the brain; it is a sensate intelligence distributed throughout the body. As with many of the more profound scientific discoveries of the twentieth century, the discovery of the neural and physiological basis of the bodymind has not had the revolutionary consequences it warrants. Most people, when asked to point to their mind, will touch their heads. As it turns out, gesturing to the head to indicate mind is about as wrongheaded as locating the soul in the Pineal gland — one of René Descartes's more notorious contributions to the history of the psyche. The *brain* is located in the head, but this is only one part of mind.

Though Descartes is the person credited with fomenting the confusion between mind and brain, he can only be held responsible in part. When he published the *Meditations* in 1641, they augmented a trend that had begun with Galileo in distinguishing reliable and measurable objects from unreliable and unmeasurable subjects. Once this distinction was articulated, it immediately became a self-evident and unchallenged Truth. To this day, the subjective is considered distinctly less real and therefore less important than the objective. With Descartes's famous dictum "I think therefore I am" (or, in the original Latin, *cogito, ergo sum*) he objectified both his capacity to think and he objectified himself as a thinking thing. For Descartes, the sum total of human being, including even the human soul, was thinking. What Descartes formulated in the *cogito* was that the awareness of a person's thinking, and awareness of the person as a thinking being, guarantees not only individual existence but God's existence, too.[145] For Descartes, "there could have been minds without bodies."[146]

This persistent error is convincingly challenged by one of America's leading neurologists, Antonio Damasio. In his research into a rare neurological condition known as "anosognosia," Damasio arrived at an important and far-reaching conclusion. It has long been known that misdirected and especially unconscious emotion can wreak havoc with reasoning abilities. Neurologists have recently discovered that the *absence* of emotion and feeling is "no less damaging, no less capable of compromising the rationality that makes us distinctively human." It is the awareness of emotion, in fact, that "allows us to decide in consonance with a sense of personal future, social convention, and moral principle."[147] Without emotion a person could use the reason required in higher math, say for instance, to solve equations using differential calculus. But people wouldn't be able to use reason to conduct their life. That kind of reasoning requires the ability to evaluate social and moral situations, which depend upon current emotional information.[148] Damasio concludes that it is simply not sensible to leave emotions and feelings out of any overall concept of mind. "I think, therefore I am" expresses the exact opposite of what Damasio and other neurologists believe to be the truth. Thinking and the awareness of thinking are *not* the real substrates of being. Likewise, it is simply wrong to imagine, as Descartes did, that thinking is separate from the body. Then why, Damasio asks, bother with this error of Descartes'? The reason is simple, he answers. For many people *Descartes's views are regarded as self-evident and in no need of reexamination.*[149]

Descartes's error took on a life of its own in the centuries since he first published his *Meditations*, and we charted some of its effect in our history of qualitative inquiry in Chapter 2. "I think, therefore I am" is a terse and articulate statement — the quintessential sound bite, perfectly suited for the modern attention span. Descartes's name is now firmly linked with cool, controlled reason, and only a few individuals understand that Cartesian philosophy is not and never can be whole natured. Both Descartes as the "new man" and his philosophy were "born of impatience with painful complexity; neither were what they claimed." [150]

Complexity is only painful to the rigid, reductive mind. As discussed in Chapter 3 and again in this chapter, the complexity that is modeled by the psyche and the cosmos is essential to wholeness. Any clarity that is achieved at the expense of complexity is rooted neither in the feelings and values that arise within the body nor in the depth of attachment that felt between lovers and the people and things they love. Someone who achieves such clarity, probably by insisting on one legitimate style of learning, knowing and being, is inclined towards fundamentalism. Though their enthusiasm may be admirable and persuasive, one should not confuse fervor for wisdom. Fundamentalists fall into the dangerous trap that L. L. Whyte identified: total obsession with partial ideas. Such people simply are incapable of the inner amplitude that leaves sufficient room for the play of many different styles of learning and being. Those who are more at ease with complexity and contradiction easily can see that clarity is naturally paired with its complements, confusion and disorientation. What is clear one moment will inevitably lose clarity the next because the psyche, like the body, is a fluid, dynamic system. For these reasons, an epistemology that relies exclusively on cold, clear, reason is antithetical to psychological inquiry and psychological life.

REALIZING THE GROUND OF CONNECTEDNESS

It is at the core of modernity to deny both the more-than-human world and to deny interconnectedness among human beings. In other words, modern people tend to ignore their place in the cosmos, including their effect on it and vulnerability to it. This narrow preoccupation with the

individual self has shaped both consciousness and culture. But as Charlene Spretnak points out, it is not necessary to invent the notion of interconnectedness — it already exists. "Interrelatedness has been expe-
rientially grasped in myriad cultural contexts and variously expressed as
the core perception of the wisdom traditions," she says. "Yet the forces of
modernity continually deny and degrade it."[151] There seems to be little
recognition of how much effort this denial takes and how much suffering
results from viewing the world as dead, inert matter lacking any connection to human life.

Realizing the ground of humanity's connectedness with the cosmos
is a practice that unites reason and passion. One feels reverence for the
immense, numinous powers of the cosmos of which human beings are an
integral part. The union of reason and passion is reminiscent of how Brian
Swimme describes the night of November 22, 1914, the moment when
Albert Einstein created his General and Special Theories of Relativity:

> To everyone alive at that time, his equation would appear to be
> just some letters and a few numbers scrawled onto the page. But to
> Einstein they revealed something unbelievable about the universe
> as a whole. Even though by this time he must have grown somewhat
> accustomed to the regularity with which shattering truths dropped
> from his fingertips, Einstein was stunned into bafflement by what
> he was seeing. Through these symbols the universe whispered that
> it was expanding in all directions. No one in three centuries of
> modern scientific work had imagined such a possibility.
>
> Psychological investigators later questioned Einstein about his
> consciousness during such moments of radical creativity, and he
> stunned them with his reply . . . Instead of speaking of algebraic
> formalisms or geometric intuitions Einstein, after reflecting on the
> question carefully, said that his experiences were of "the muscular
> type" . . . Chock-full with the very dynamics he sat contemplating,
> Einstein experienced a birth that permeated him whole, his mind,
> his muscles, his viscera.[152]

Einstein's consciousness at the moment of his discovery of the field
equations is a wonderful expression of the mind that permeates body.

Describing his consciousness as "muscular" is startling, though. Some may assume that a person of Einstein's genius would be pure intellect, a kind of walking and talking head. The idea that genius is in, and of, the body is contrary to some ideas about human creativity. Yet it is wholly compatible with a psychological understanding of creativity because the spontaneous, embodied experience of new ideas is only one way the complex psyche expresses its dynamic nature.

It also is important to note that Einstein was prepared to take part in the self-revelation of the cosmos. Years of dedication to the art and craft of mathematics and physics made it possible to see through the givens of his Newtonian inheritance, and discover the deeper dynamics of the universe. Yes, Einstein received its shattering truths through his entire "muscular" organism. But these shattering truths did not simply drop from uneducated or unprepared fingertips. Einstein was truly a master because he had devoted years to apprenticeship. True mastery — not the synonym for "control" which is what so often passes for mastery these days — always does.

Reflection upon Einstein's discovery that November night in 1914 suggests a connection to the Jewish mystical tradition called Kabbalah. There is a distinct beauty to the tradition partly revealed by what the word Kabbalah means: *receiving*, or *that which has been received*. Daniel Matt, who is an expert on Kabbalah, says that this refers to both the received tradition as well as the gifts of wisdom that arrive spontaneously and unexpectedly when people are truly receptive.[153] Deep souls, according to the *Zohar*, hide themselves from consciousness. But when one dedicates oneself to soul, she will reveal herself "spangling a few sparkles of her light." To do this, people must "gather everything, without hatred, jealously, or rivalry."[154] This emphasis on gathering instead of transcendence expresses something that can be forgotten so easily: the immanence of the divine. "Do not say, 'This is a stone and not God.' God forbid! Rather, all existence is God, and the stone is a thing pervaded by divinity."[155] Reverence for all living things is transformative, according to *Zohar*, for it is then that

> The light of peace and a fierce boldness manifest in you. The splendor of compassion and the glory of love shine through you. The

desire to act and work, the passion to create and to restore yourself, the yearning for silence and for the inner shout of joy — these all band together in your spirit, and you become holy.[156]

Reverence for all living things includes reverence for the soul, realized most intimately and urgently in the passion to create and restore ourselves. Without the actor, no action is possible; without the worker, no work is possible. It begins with the individual who has the capacity to act, work, and create and who, paradoxically, *becomes* an individual through acting, working, and creating. Who would not want to be "great souled," to manifest the light of peace and fierce boldness? Who would not want to be smack in the center of their own dynamic *becoming* — both the lump of clay on the wheel *and* the potter who centers and shapes that lump with loving attention? And yet this paradoxical combination of shaping and being shaped is a peculiar and counter-cultural notion of heroism. To actively participate in one's own individuation requires balancing an intentional, assertive *yang* posture alongside a receptive, fluid *yin* posture.

Let us return again to the image of the divine child and the play of give-and-take that is such a prominent part of childhood. To remember the divine child is to recall one's necessary participation in becoming, since the child is the archetype of futurity. Making one's way back to the child is the critical step, and this chapter has suggested some ways to do this. When all is said and done, it begins with simple willingness to receive what the child has to teach and revere the curious, playful, adventurous spirit of the child. Once this occurs, the power of the divine child makes it impossible to do anything but become a unique self. Jung writes:

> The divine child is a personification of vital forces quite outside the limited range of our conscious mind; of ways and possibilities of which our one-sided conscious mind knows nothing: a wholeness which embraces the very depths of Nature. It represents the strongest, the most ineluctable urge in every being, namely the urge to realize itself. It is, as it were, an incarnation of the inability to do otherwise, equipped with all the powers of nature and instinct.[157]

The ineluctable vital force of the child has much in common with the vital expansion of the cosmos. Both child and cosmos are fluid, dynamic, and complex. Imagine them as eager participants in their own self-realization. Perhaps they share these qualities with the psyche, which suggests the psyche's desire to realize itself. Certainly the original images and first stories about the psyche reinforce this idea. The psyche was often portrayed as a butterfly, the end result of an inexorable transformation from caterpillar to chrysalis to butterfly. In the Greco-Roman myth *Eros and Psyche*, Psyche is a young woman who is driven to participate in her own transformation, painful and humiliating as this journey is. Perhaps the self-realization of Psyche is the true purpose of psychological life.

DEPTH OF FIELD AND THE PLENITUDE OF PSYCHE

Psychologists of the unconscious including Freud, Jung and their followers tend to think of depth as verticality. One looks for layers of meaning beneath or below the surface of something to understand its full symbolic richness. We have spoken about this many times ourselves in the preceding chapters. Upon reflection, another idea presents itself that contradicts the assumption that depth is vertical and the direction of the psyche is always downward toward a fathomless bottom. Depth is also a measure of the horizontal distance between one thing and another. Photographers call it "depth of field" and it is an important factor they take into account when setting up an image. For instance, Ansel Adam's images of Yosemite have great depth of field. Objects in the foreground, middle, and background are equally clear and distinct. This permits the human eye to see the whole field at one time, roaming over a two-dimensional representation as if one were actually there, standing at the artist's side, equally captivated by the three-dimensional reality.

The ability to perceive depth of field reveals the paradoxical nexus between the particular and the universal, the part and the whole. As awareness of the distinct features of the world grows, one begins to perceive one's own distinctiveness. Yet both self and other are viewed within the context of the entire landscape, with human complexity simply mirroring the complexity of the universe. This is differentiation without disengagement, for the gap between self and other is charged with eros. Perception is tinged with desire; relationships between phenomena form the ground of connectedness. Thus horizontal depth of field, like its cousin vertical depth, can foster a genuine reverence for complexity and diversity. Not only does it permit *perception* of the concrete, the particular, and the individual; it can foster an *appreciation* of it too. Perceiving depth of the field is a kind of initiation into one's dynamic connectedness with every feature and phenomenon of the anima mundi. People can play within this dynamic by continually shifting awareness to see the forest for the trees and the trees that make up the forest.

Appreciating the depth of field in the *anima mundi* requires receptivity to what presents itself as truly other, displaying the sharp or subtle differences that so easily foster alienation and antagonism. When another person challenges one's cherished ideas and beliefs, receptivity is difficult. It is far easier to put up resistance and feel a creeping rigidity in mind and body. Such rigidity makes play impossible. Or, it transforms play into a deadly earnest competition characterized by domination or subjugation of the other. What might happen if one were to allow meaning, knowledge, and insight to arise within the context of such adversarial relationships instead? What might be possible if one were able to see opponents as teachers?

It is possible to relax into an appreciation of difference not only in contemplative solitude, but in community, with adversaries as well as with allies, or amidst the clutter and chatter of modern technological life. One environment does not hold the psyche more so than another does. Psyche is not necessarily more present in the wilderness, or during meditation, or in moments of despair and melancholy. By acknowledging her reality and autonomy, one awakens to Psyche's absolute freedom to manifest herself in countless ways. In psychological life, Psyche is anywhere and everywhere.

The psyche's ubiquitous presence and full reality grants new insights into the meaning of home. In Chapter 3, we spoke about the odyssey of research and compared the inquiring person to the archetypal journeyer, whose situation is defined by movement and fluctuation. What does it mean to be a journeyer in life and not just for the duration of a creative project? Consider what Kerényi says. "The journeyer is at home while underway, at home on the road itself," he declares. The road isn't a literal pathway between two places; instead, it is its own world that is naturally open to everywhere. The journeyer gives meaning to the road just as the road gives meaning to the journey. They form, as it were, "a world in its own right, a middle domain, where a person has access to everything."[158]

Both the journeyer and the child symbolize the allure of the unknown and the willingness to be guided down unexpected paths. It is just these qualities that are essential to psychological inquiry and to living a psychological life. Because the archetypal journeyer is an adult, not an infant or child, this figure serves an important purpose. It suggests that one need not abandon childlike curiosity no matter how long or how far the journey. One can be at home while journeying and the journey can become a home in the fullest possible sense of that word. Perhaps the true journeyer finds sanctuary in movement more than stillness, in surrender more than control, in engagement more than isolation, in discovery more than certainty, and in longing more than satiety. If the figure of the journeyer is at the center of psychological life, perhaps our task is simply to be true to Psyche, making a home for her wherever we happen to be.

NOTES

1. *The Collected Dialogues of Plato,* Hamilton, Edith and Huntington Cairns, eds. (Princeton: Princeton University Press, 1961), p. 16.

2. Ibid., p. 23.

3. Ibid., p. 524.

4 Baring, Anne and Jules Cashford, *The Myth of the Goddess: Evolution of an Image* (New York: Arkana/Penguin., 1991), p. 609. For a full discussion of the history of *sophia* in her many guises, read the section on the origins of *sophia* (pp. 471–478) and ch. 15.

5. Ibid., p. 473.

6 Rilke, Rainer Maria, *Letters to a Young Poet,* S. Mitchell, trans. (Boston: Shambhala, 1993), pp. 23–24.

7. Freud, Sigmund, *New Introductory Lectures in Psycho-Analysis,* J. Strachey, trans. (New York: W. W. Norton & Company, 1965), p. 196.

8. Ibid, pp. 99–100.

9. Auden, W. H., "In Memory of Sigmund Freud" in *Collected Poems,* (New York: Random House, 1976), p. 217.

10. *The Collected Dialogues of Plato,* p. 7.

11. Victor Frankl articulated this question in his remarkable account of surviving a World War II concentration camp, *Man's Search For Meaning.*

12. Jung, C. G., *Collected Works,* vol. 6: *Psychological Types,* Bollingen Series XX (Princeton: Princeton University Press, 1990), p. 448.

13. Whitmont, Edward C., *The Symbolic Quest* (Princeton, NJ: Princeton University Press, 1991), p. 175.

14. Rilke, *Letters,* pp. 88–89.

15. Ibid., p. 90.

16. von Franz, Marie-Louise, *Alchemy* (Toronto: Inner City Books, 1980), pp. 144–145.

17. We borrow this phrase from James Hillman, who discusses pathologizing, personifying, and psychologizing as natural activities of the soul
in *Revisioning Psychology* (New York: Harper Colophon Books, 1975). We
notice that each of these natural activities of the soul is a form of inquiry since all of them can be rendered as a specific question. For instance,
when the soul personifies it asks the question, "Who's here?" When it
pathologizes it asks, "What's wrong?" When it psychologizes, the soul
wants to know, "What does it mean?"

18. Romanyshyn, Robert D., "The Orphan and the Angel," *Psychological
Perspectives* 32 (1995), p. 98.

19. In a later chapter we will examine this idea of a mythic sense as
practice of scholarly inquiry. For now it is important to see that it is way
of criticizing the absolutist approach to knowing without depreciating
the importance of knowing. We all know how important our myths are
to how we see the world. A psychological approach to knowing takes
this into account and places myth and fact on a similar footing regarding validity.

20. Wheelwright, Philip Ellis, *Heraclitus* (Princeton, NJ: Princeton University Press, 1959), p. 59.

21. Denzin, Norman K. and Yvonna S. Lincoln, *Handbook of Qualitative
Research,* (Thousand Oaks, CA: Sage Publications, 1994), pp. 6–11.

22. L. L. Whyte, *The Unconscious Before Freud* (London: Julian Freedman,
1979), pp. 7–8; original italics.

23. Wheelright, *Heraclitus,* p. 64.

24. Jung, C. G., *Collected Works,* vol. 9.2: *Aion,* Bollingen Series XX (Princeton: Princeton University Press, 1978), p. 261.

25. Quoted in Gay, Peter, *The Freud Reader* (New York: W. W. Norton &
Company, 1989), p. 573.

26. Ibid., pp. 563–64.

27. Freud, Sigmund, *An Outline of Psycho-Analysis,* J. Strachey, trans. (New
York: W. W. Norton & Company, 1949), p. 68.

28. Ibid., p. 66.

29. Quoted in Edinger, Edward, *Ego and Archetype* (Boston: Shambhala,
1985), p. 115.

30. Jung, C. G., *Collected Works,* vol. 17: *The Development of Personality,* Bollingen Series XX (Princeton: Princeton University Press, 1954), p. 179.

31. Stevens, Anthony, *On Jung* (London: Routledge, 1990), p. 204.

32. Jung, C. G., *Collected Works*, vol. 8: *The Structure and Dynamics of the Psyche*, Bollingen Series xx (Princeton: Princeton University Press, 1981), p. 137.

33. Hillman, *Revisioning Psychology*, p. xiv.

34. Ibid., p. 131.

35. Roth, Michael S., ed., *Freud: Conflict and Culture* (New York: Vintage Books, 1998), p. ix.

36. Mitchell, Stephen A. and Margaret J. Black, *Freud and Beyond: A History of Modern Psychoanalytic Thought* (New York: Basic Books, 1995), pp. xviii, xvix.

37. Hillman, *Revisioning Psychology*, p. xiv.

38. Ibid., p. xiv.

39. Ibid., p. xvi.

40. Ibid., p. xvi.

41. Ibid., pp. 206–07.

42. Ibid., p. 68.

43. Ibid., pp. xiv, xvi.

44. Abram, David, *The Spell of the Sensuous: Perception and Language in a More-Than-Human World* (New York: Vintage Books, 1996), p. 58.

45. Hillman, *Revisioning Psychology*, pp. 141–42.

46 Ibid., p. 142.

47. Romanyshyn, Robert D., *Technology As Symptom and Dream* (London: Routledge, 1989), p. 140.

48. Freud, *An Outline of Psycho-Analysis*, p. 50.

49. Hillman, *Revisioning Psychology*, p. 2.

50. In his 1982 book *Freud and Man's Soul*, Bruno Bettelheim argues that the English translations of Freud have fostered this emphasis by virtually eliminating soul from his language. The Standard Edition translates *Seele*, which is German for soul or psyche, as "mind." In other words, whenever the words "mind" or "mental," or the phrase "mental functioning," appear in Freud's works, says Bettelheim, readers should consider the alternate translations of "psyche," "psychic," and "psychic functioning" with their undertones of soul.

51. Jung, *Aion*, p. 261.

52. Jung, *Psychological Types,* p. 448.

53. Hillman, James, *Anima: Anatomy of a Personified Notion* (Dallas: Spring Publications, 1985), p. 108.

54. Kerényi, Karl, *Hermes: Guide of Souls,* Murray Stein, trans. (Woodstock, CT: Spring Publications, 1996), pp. 44–46.

55. Freud, *New Introductory Lectures in Psycho-Analysis,* p. 72.

56. Ibid., p. 120.

57. Freud, *An Outline of Psycho-Analysis,* p. 31.

58. "Psychological Aspects of the Mother Archetype" in *Collected Works,* vol. 9.1, Bollingen Series XX (Princeton: Princeton University Press, 1990), p. 96.

59. von Franz, Marie-Louise, *An Introduction to the Psychology of Fairy Tales* (New York: Spring Publications, 1970), p. 6.

60. Samuels, Andrew, *Jung and the Post-Jungians* (London: Routledge, 1985), p. 29.

61. Hillman, James, *The Myth of Analysis: Three Essays in Archetypal Psychology* (Evanston, Ill.: Northwestern University Press, 1972), pp. 80–82.

62. Hillman, *Revisioning Psychology,* p. 55.

63. Freud, *New Introductory Lectures in Psycho-Analysis,* p. 71.

64. Romanyshyn, Robert D., *Technology as Symptom and Dream* (London: Routledge, 1989), p. 205.

65. Ibid., p. 13.

66. Hillman, James (1992), *The Thought of the Heart and the Soul of the World* (Dallas: Spring Publications, 1992), p. 43.

67. quoted in Gay, *The Freud Reader,* p. 574.

68. quoted in ibid., p. 635.

69. Hillman, *Anima: Anatomy of a Personified Notion,* p. x.

70. Corbett, Lionel, *The Religious Function of the Psyche* (London: Routledge, 1996), pp. 98–99.

71. Hillman, James, *Insearch: Psychology and Religion* (Woodstock, CT: Spring Publications, 1994), pp. 53–54.

72. Jung, C. G., *Collected Works,* vol. 14: *Mysterium coniunctionis,* Bollingen Series XX (Princeton: Princeton University Press, 1989), p. 472.

73. Ibid., p. 489.

74. Hillman, *Revisioning Psychology,* pp. 57–58.

75. Jung, *Mysterium coniunctionis,* p. 528.

76. Jung, C. G., *Memories, Dreams, Reflections* (New York: Vintage Books, 1989), p. 45.

77. Whether or not Diotema was a living person is still a source of some controversy among scholars.

78. Jung, C. G., *Collected Works,* vol. 12: *Psychology and Alchemy,* Bollingen Series XX (Princeton: Princeton University Press, 1993), p. 276.

79. Jung, C. G., *Collected Works,* vol. 13: *Alchemical Studies,* Bollingen Series XX (Princeton: Princeton University Press, 1983), pp. 47–48.

80. Hillman, *Insearch,* p. 43; emphasis added.

81. Watkins, Mary, *Invisible Guests: The Development of Imaginal Dialogues* (Boston: Sigo Press, 1986), pp. 102–03.

82. Hillman, *Revisioning Psychology,* p. 106.

83. Jung, *Memories, Dreams, Reflections,* p. 183.

84. Ibid., p. 184.

85. Jung, C. G., *Collected Works,* vol. 8: *The Structure and Dynamics of the Psyche,* Bollingen Series XX (Princeton: Princeton University Press, 1981), p. 157.

86. Downing, Christine, *The Goddess: Mythological Images of the Feminine* (New York: Crossroad, 1981), p. 2.

87. Freud, *An Outline of Psycho-Analysis,* p. 15.

88. Freud, *New Introductory Lectures in Psycho-Analysis,* p. 178.

89. Freud, *An Outline of Psycho-Analysis,* p. 16.

90. Freud, *New Introductory Lectures in Psycho-Analysis,* p. 73.

91. Jung, C. G., *Collected Works,* vol. 7: *Two Essays in Analytical Psychology,* Bollingen Series XX (Princeton: Princeton University Press, 1972), p. 201.

92. Jung, C. G., *Collected Works,* vol. 11: *Psychology and Religion,* Bollingen Series XX (Princeton: Princeton University Press, 1989), pp. 13–14.

93. Whitmont, *The Symbolic Quest,* p. 69.

94. von Franz, *Alchemy,* p. 44.

95. This idea was discussed in Chapter 1, where we cited two of the dialogues of Plato, the *Apology* (23a) and the *Phaedrus* (278d), as instances in which Socrates describes the unbridgeable gap between humankind and the gods. Another dialogue that reiterates this theme is the *Symposium,* where Socrates says "the divine will not mingle directly with the human,

and it is only through the mediation of the spirit world that man can have any intercourse, whether waking or sleeping, with the gods" (203a), in *The Collected Dialogues of Plato*, p. 555.

96. Giegerich, Wolfgang, *The Soul's Logical Life: Towards a Rigorous Notion of Psychology* (New York-Frankfurt/M: 1998), p. 133.

97. Quoted in Palmer, Richard, E., *Hermeneutics* (Evanston, Ill.: Northwestern University Press, 1969), p. 164.

98. Jung, C.G. "Psychological Aspects of the Mother Archetype," pp. 75–110.

99. Moore, Thomas, *The Planets Within: The Astrological Psychology of Marsilio Ficino* (Hudson, NY: Lindisfarne Press, 1982), p. 37.

100. Edinger, *Ego and Archetype*, p. 137.

101. von Franz, *Alchemy*, pp. 144–45.

102. Moore, *The Planets Within*, pp. 37–38.

103. Moore, Thomas, *Care of the Soul: A Guide for Cultivating Depth and Sacredness in Everyday Life* (New York: HarperCollins, 1992), p. xviii.

104. Mamet, David, *Three Uses of the Knife: On the Nature and Purpose of Drama* (New York: Vintage Books), p. 68.

105. Adolf Guggenbühl-Craig discusses this idea in several places in his book *Power in the Helping Professions* (Zurich: Spring Publications, 1971), see specifically the chapter entitled "Eros," pp. 135–137.

106. Freud, Sigmund, *A General Introduction to Psycho-Analysis* (Garden City, NY: Garden City Publishing, 1943), p. 256: ". . . the patient knows how to set up resistances within the boundaries of analysis proper, and the defeat of these is one of the most difficult tasks of the technique. Instead of remembering certain of the feelings and states of mind of his previous life, he reproduces them, lives through again such of them as, by means of what is called the 'transference,' may be made effective in opposition against the physician and the treatment."

107. Romanyshyn, Robert D. and Goodchild, Veronica, *Doing Research with Soul in Mind: The Alchemical Hermeneutic Method* (forthcoming).

108. Ibid.

109. Ibid.

110. Ibid.

111. For more information about the dialogue process, see David Bohm's book, *On Dialogue* (London: Routledge, 1996).

112. Hillman, James, *Emotion* (Evanston, Ill.: Northwestern University Press, 1960), pp. 362, 283.

113. Chalquist, Craig, *In the Shadow of Cross and Sword: Imagining a Psychoanalysis of Place*. PhD diss., Pacifica Graduate Institute, 2000.

114. Reason, Peter and John Rowan, *Human Inquiry: A Sourcebook of New Paradigm Research* (Chichester, England: John Wiley & Sons, 1981), p. 114.

115. Ibid.

116. Moustakas, Clark, *Heuristic Research: Design, Methodology, and Applications* (Newbury Park, CA: Sage Publications, 1990), p. 24.

117. We are choosing to use "language" and "words" somewhat interchangeably here which from a linguistic perspective would be both incorrect and unhelpful. There are valuable distinctions in terms of function and we encourage a critical appraisal of our choice here. However, we consider both terms as referring to animate phenomena, which are also both mistakenly used as inanimate tools. As that is our primary concern here we are choosing to use the both word in the same way.

118. Hillman, *Revisioning Psychology*, p. 217.

119. Hillman discusses this in Part 2 of the book, entitled "On psychological language."

120. Freud's *A General Introduction to Psycho-Analysis* contains three lectures on the psychology of errors (pp. 17–71).

121. Jung, C. G., *Collected Works*, vol. 2: *Experimental Researches*, Bollingen Series XX (Princeton: Princeton University Press, 1981).

122. Stevens, *On Jung*, p. 180.

123. Moore, *The Planets Within*, p. 33.

124. Ibid., p. 44.

125. Bradbury, Ray, *Zen in the Art of Writing* (New York, Bantam Books, 1992), p. 4.

126. Field, Reshad, *The Invisible Way: A Journey into Conscious Loving and Dying* (New York: Harper & Row, 1976), p. 18.

127. Polanyi, Michael, *Knowing and Being* (Chicago: University of Chicago Press, 1969), p. 118.

128. Quoted in Moustakas, *Heuristic Research*, p. 41.

129. Braud, William and Rosemarie Anderson, *Transpersonal Research Methods for the Social Sciences: Honoring Human Experience* (Thousand Oaks, CA: SAGE Publications, 1998), pp. 69–93.

130. See Glaser, Barney G., and Anselm L. Strauss, *The Discovery of Grounded Theory: Strategies For Qualitative Research* (Hawthorne, NY: Aldine de Gruyter, 1967) for a full description of this method.

131. Braud and Anderson, *Transpersonal Research*, p. 73ff.

132. Nelson, Victoria, *On Writer's Block: A New Approach to Creativity* (New York: Houghton-Mifflin, 1993), p. 103.

133. Jung, C.G., *Collected Works*, vol. 15: *The Spirit in Man, Art, and Literature*, Bollingen Series XX (Princeton: Princeton University Press, 1966), p. 103.

134. Jung, C.G., *Collected Works*, vol. 9.1: *The Archetypes of the Collective Unconscious*, Bollingen Series XX (Princeton: Princeton University Press, 1990), p. 164.

135. Jung, *Mysterium coniunctionis*, p. 533.

136. Jung, *The Archetypes of the Collective Unconscious*, p. 120.

137. Swimme, Brian, *The Hidden Heart of the Cosmos: Humanity and the New Story* (Maryknoll, NY: Orbis Books, 1996), pp. 35, 42.

138. Jung, *Psychology and Religion*, p. 105.

139. Bachelard, Gaston, *The Poetics of Reverie* (New York: Orion Press, 1969), p. 53.

140. Hillman, *The Thought of the Heart and the Soul of the World*, pp. 115–21.

141. Ibid., p. 213.

142. Ibid., p. 222.

143. Ibid., p. 232.

144. von Franz, Marie-Louise, *Dreams* (Boston: Shambhala, 1991), pp. 123, 154.

145. Taylor, Charles, *Sources of the Self: The Making of the Modern Identity* (Cambridge, MA: Harvard University Press, 1989), pp. 187–88.

146. Damasio, Antonio, *Descartes' Error: Emotion, Reason, and the Human Brain* (New York: G.P. Putnam's Sons, 1994), p. xii.

147. The anosognosic patients that Damasio works with have an impaired ability to process current body states. Their minds rely on old information, which grows older by the minute, with the result that "the state of self that they are able to construct is thus impoverished" (p. 237). These patients lack what Damasio calls a "background feeling" that corresponds to the body state prevailing between strong emotions. It is

"our image of the body landscape when it is not shaken by emotions" and without it, the "very core" of our "representation of self would be broken." This landscape, this biological basis of the self, is "a composite, ongoing representation of current body states that is "distributed over a large number of structures in both subcortical and cortical locations . . . Such an ongoing, unstoppable representation of the body state" Damasio says, "is what allows you to reply promptly to the specific question 'How do you feel?'" (pp. 150–52).

148. Ibid., p. 250.

149. Whyte, L. L., *The Unconscious Before Freud,* pp. 87–88.

150. Spretnak, Charlene, *States of Grace: Spiritual Grounding in the Postmodern Age* (San Francisco: HarperSanFrancisco, 1991), pp. 156, 188.

151. Swimme, *The Hidden Heart of the Cosmos,* pp. 71, 106–108.

152. Matt, Daniel C., *The Essential Kabbalah: The Heart of Jewish Mysticism* (San Francisco: HarperSanFrancisco, 1996), p. 1.

153. Ibid., p. 124.

154. Ibid., p. 24.

155. Ibid., p. 124.

156. Jung, *The Archetypes of the Collective Unconscious,* p. 170.

157. Kerényi, *Hermes,* pp. 44–46.

ACKNOWLEDGMENTS

We are deeply grateful to many people who have contributed their time, their energy, and their imagination to our project. To begin, we want to acknowledge our students who have, over the past ten years, helped us articulate the challenges of doing inquiry that is guided by the psyche. We learned from them as we were writing for them, and their thoughtful, enthusiastic response enriched the book immeasurably.

It will be obvious that this book owes much to the work of familiar figures in the field of psychology. We rely extensively upon the writings of both Freud and Jung to frame the theoretical backdrop of our ideas about the psyche and about doing psychologically oriented work. But we have been even more explicitly guided by the work of James Hillman whose re-examination of depth psychology has done so much to move it from the clinical setting into the world, where soul as a perspective offers fresh insights into culture, history, and society. James has been our teacher and our colleague and this book would not be possible without him.

We are also indebted to Robert Romanyshyn whose psychologically enriched approach to research has provided so much stimulus through the years. The threads of his work both hold and color the weave of ours in a way that has been essential. Other colleagues who have inspired us include Mary Watkins, Erik Craig, Veronica Goodchild, Glen Slater, Dennis Slattery, and Ginette Paris, all of whom have written and lectured on depth psychological ways of knowing. We were supported also by Richard Tarnas who was kind enough to read an early draft and gave us valuable feedback.

We are both immensely grateful for the continual support and enthusiasm of Christine Downing, who read and critiqued early drafts. It is a better book by far for her editorial comments.

We thank Sara Coppin, Erin Coppin, and Geoffrey Gottlieb, all of whom burned the midnight oil on many occasions reading and editing the manuscript. Their talents and their grace under pressure polished this work into a form we now feel ready to release.

This second edition has been edited by Klaus Ottmann, editor-in-chief at Spring Publications, and we are grateful for his help, particularly in assisting with the construction of an index, which was notably missing in the first edition. Others, including Steve Aizenstat, Charles Asher, Carla Gilbert, and Rosemarie Anderson, have provided criticism and support for the changes we have made in this edition.

INDEX

A

Abram, David 50
Academic research 127
Academic writing 9, 110
Adler, Alfred 43
Alchemy 58, 79, 105
    alchemical hermeneutic method 168 n. 107
    alchemical process es of inquiry 105
Analytical Psychology 64
Anderson, Rosemarie 133, 138, 169
Anima mundi 8, 52, 66, 70, 151, 161
Apollo 41, 78
Archetypal 48–49, 56, 58–59, 71, 74, 78–79, 101, 103
    child 9, 11, 145–47
    eros 125
    image 59
    nature of psychological inquiry 101
    psychology 49, 58, 71, 82, 93
    journeyer 161–62
Archetype 46–49, 59, 64, 78, 159
Ares 48
Aristotle 93
Aspects of the psyche 31, 57, 101
Associative language of image 20
Attitude toward research
    anticipation 94
    informed inquiry 124
    inquiring 122
Auden, W. H. 17
Authentic voice 121
Autonomous images 96

J

Janet, Pierre 76
Jung, C. G.
  and depth psychology 43
  classical Jungian theory 58
  Jung's analytical psychology 64
  Jung's idea of the psyche 73
  Jung's theory of the archetypes 58

K

Kabbalah 158, 171
Kant, Immanuel 25–27, 33, 80, 126
Kepler, Johann 24
Kerényi, Karl 55, 162

L

Libido 43, 56–57, 59
Lincoln, Yvonna S. 34–37
Lived experience
  of a dialectical psyche 30
  of inquiry 146
  context of 89
Locianalysis 103
Logos of method 89
Love 11–13, 21, 60, 116, 126, 152, 158
  as a quest 12
  and eros 60

M

Mamet, David 96, 168
Malinowski, Bronislaw 34
Mental processes 26, 43
Merleau-Ponty, Maurice 33
Method 37–38, 89–90, 92, 99, 128, 131–135
  of inquiry 33
  versus move 89–90

T

Tarnas, Richard 150
Taylor, Charles 43, 152–153
Telos 8, 54, 80, 82, 147
Transference 74, 90, 98–101, 119–120, 131, 138, 140

U

Unconscious 42–45
  collective 54

V

Verstehen 29
Volkspsychologie 31
von Franz, Marie-Louise 20, 77, 92, 147, 163

W

Watkins, Mary 71, 167
Weltanschauung 15, 64, 77
Wheelright, Philip 40
Whitmont, Edward 18
Whyte, L. L. 40, 86, 156
Wundt, Wilhelm 31

Y

Yang 11, 13, 15, 40, 147, 159
  posture of inquiry 15, 147
Yin 11, 13–15, 40, 59, 102, 147, 159
  posture of inquiry 59

Z

Zoha r 158

ABOUT THE AUTHORS

JOSEPH COPPIN has been a psychotherapist in the tradition of depth psychology for twenty-five years. His training and background in Freudian, Jungian, and archetypal psychology have blended clinical experiences with teaching, writing, research, and consultation. He has been the Chair of the Depth Psychology Program and is now Research Coordinator of the Clinical Psychology program at Pacifica Graduate Institute.

ELIZABETH NELSON earned her doctorate in depth psychology in 2001. She has degrees in economics, political science, and literature and more than twenty years of business experience as a writer/editor for clients in technology, health, and finance. Currently she is a book coach for aspiring authors and conducts seminars on writing and publishing. She is full-time faculty at the Art Institute of California and adjunct faculty at Pacifica Graduate Institute, teaching depth psychology, philosophy, story writing, and research methodology.